Make Me a
STORY

Make Me a
STORY

Teaching Writing Through Digital Storytelling

Lisa C. Miller

Foreword by Linda Rief

Stenhouse PUBLISHERS

Portland, Maine

Stenhouse Publishers
www.stenhouse.com

CREDITS

Front cover photo: Christian Kretz, iStockphoto.

Make Me a Story: Teaching Writing Through Digital Storytelling is an independent publication and is not affiliated with, nor has it been authorized, sponsored, or otherwise approved by, Microsoft Corporation.

TEXT

Pages 61–77: Microsoft Digital Story 3 screen shots reprinted with permission from Microsoft Corporation.

Pages 81–83: Standards for the English Language Arts, by the International Reading Association and the National Council of Teachers of English, Copyright 1996 by the International Reading Association and the National Council of Teachers of English. Used with permission.

Pages 83–84: NETS for Students: National Educational Technology Standards for Students, Second Edition 2007, ISTE © [International Society for Technology in Education], www.iste.org. All rights reserved. Used with permission.

Page 87: Digital Storytelling Rubric by Kevin Hodgson, http://www.umass.edu/wmwp/
DigitalStorytelling/Rubric%20Assessment.htm. Used by permission.

CD

Addax: Sahara Conservation Fund image © Sahara Conservation Fund, www.saharaconservation.org. Used by permission.

Baby addax Safiya and Fola at the Louisville Zoo. Photograph © Kara Bussabarger/Louisville Zoo. Used by permission of the Louisville Zoo, www.louisvillezoo.org.

Addax range map © Brent Huffman, www.ultimateungulate.com. All rights reserved. Used by permission.

Adult addax photo © Kenneth W. Fink/National Audubon Society Collection. Used by permission of Photo Researchers, Inc.

Colby: Photographs of tornadoes used with permission of photographer Gene Rhoden.

Leo: Photograph of bearded dragon used with permission of photographer Sharon Maguire.

Cover design, interior design, and typesetting by woodwarddesign

Library of Congress Cataloging-in-Publication Data
Miller, Lisa C.
  Make me a story : teaching writing through digital storytelling / Lisa C. Miller ; Foreword by Linda Rief.
     p. cm.
  Includes bibliographical references.
  ISBN 978-1-57110-789-3 (alk. paper)
  1. Storytelling--Computer network resources. 2. Oral communication--Digital techniques. 3. Digital communications. I. Title.
  LB1042.M46 2010
  372.67'70785--dc22
                              2010015935
Manufactured in the United States of America

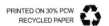 PRINTED ON 30% PCW
RECYCLED PAPER

16 15 14 13 12 11 10   9 8 7 6 5 4 3 2 1

For Don

Contents

Foreword

By Linda Rief

Last October I was on my way to a yard sale in Rowley, Massachusetts, with my son and his family. Harrison, my eight-year-old grandson, was riding with me. Earlier in the week I had noticed that Harrison had a lump on his head and a black eye. "What happened?" I asked him. Harrison told me how he had found a skateboard at the recycling center and set up a ramp in the barn to test it out. He explained what had happened as he tested out the skateboard. It was a great story, filled with his joy at finding a free skateboard, the exhilaration of the jump, and the *thwack* and *slap* as his entire contraption fell apart when he tried to skate down the ramp on the barn stairs.

As we rode in the car that day I asked him, "Did you write down that story about the skateboard you told me last week?"

"No," he said. But within seconds he had pulled out his iPod touch and begun typing rapidly with his thumbs. I wasn't sure what he was doing until he said, "Done. Want to hear it?" He read the story to me as I drove.

THE SKATEBOARD

Chapter 1
I was just going to the dump when this all started. It turned into a monster. I was now at the dump. Yes, just looking at the swap shop. I had seen two nice UNH Wildcats basketballs, so I took them. Then when my dad went to empty some oil, he saw it—the thing that I was waiting for, an old skateboard, so . . . [He read this as "so, dot dot dot."]

Chapter 2
So, as you probably know, what any kid would do is take it home with them, so I did just like any kid would do. When I got home I went out to the barn. I skateboarded for at least an hour then my mom and dad came and said that

I was going out to dinner right when I was getting all the stuff in the right spot. Something popped in my mind. I wanted to do one last trick. So I was doing the trick and the skateboard flung up into my head and that is how I got the lump and mark on my eye.

"Harrison, I really like the part where you said the experience turned into a 'monster,' and that you did what any kid would do if he found a skateboard at the recycling center: 'take it home.' I like the way you kept us in suspense by not telling us what happened until Chapter 2. I also love the way you said 'something popped' in your mind.

"You know the part where you said you put 'all the stuff in the right spot'? I was wondering what kind of contraption or ramp you built and how you placed it on the stairs. I was also wondering what it felt like, or what you were thinking, as you tried to do the trick and the skateboard flung up into your eye. Do you think you might want to add that information to the piece?"

"Not really," he said. (So much for moving the story forward with an eight-year-old, I thought.)

"Well, I would love a copy of your skateboard story just as it is."

He clicked the iPod keys a couple of times and said, "Done!" The story was waiting for me in my e-mail inbox when I returned home.

Harrison's iPod touch made it possible for him to write his story right there in the car, and the e-mail function allowed him to send his work to me (and potentially others) easily and quickly. However, the story didn't go where it could have gone if Harrison were in a class taught by a teacher who had read Lisa Miller's book, *Make Me a Story: Teaching Writing Through Digital Storytelling.*

When Lisa's editor, Toby Gordon, asked me if I would be interested in reading *Make Me a Story* and writing a foreword for it, I asked, "Are you sure you want me to do this? I know nothing about digital *anything.*" After reading this book, however,

I realize I am the person to whom this book is addressed—the teacher who is intimidated by the prospect of incorporating technology into her classroom but is open to the possibilities.

I will never catch up with my students. I will never be as fluent as they are with these twenty-first-century tools. And I will never catch up with Harrison. He will always be far ahead of me when it comes to using technology as a natural way to tell his stories. But if I want to continue to teach, I have to learn how to use some of the tools my students are using. I must be open to learning. In the past I've been totally intimidated by technology—afraid to use it if I didn't know enough about it. All of these technologies that seem to change daily are frightening. I often don't know what I should even try to learn. What tool should I use? Where do I begin? Will it be outdated before I've learned it?

Frank Smith admonished us years ago to let kids into the "literacy club" via real reading and writing, and now I have to join the twenty-first-century version of the club. At the very least, I have to let my students show me (and teach me) how they use these tools to enhance their learning.

I'm not surprised when students forget to bring pens or pencils to class—those are no longer the tools that come to mind when I ask them to write. Reading methods have changed as well. Paul, one of my eighth graders, carries all of his books in his backpack—on his Kindle. Another student, Charlie, can find definitions, synonyms, and histories of any word we have a question about in a matter of seconds using his cell phone, long before any other student could locate the dictionary or thesaurus on a shelf in the room (if they even know the answers can be found in a book).

We have to remind ourselves constantly, however, that the focus in our classrooms is reading and writing. The focus is not technology. The *tool* does not deliver the meaning; the tool may enhance the meaning and make it more engaging, but we cannot let technology itself be the message. Lisa Miller shows us that the message— the writing—is what matters. Digital stories are built on the writing and thinking that students do.

Lisa shows us how to teach writing, but she also shows us that writing is enhanced and becomes more engaging to both the writer and the audience when it is delivered through a digital medium. This is the world in which our students live. They have grown up with technology, which makes them fearless with these tools. This is what Don Murray taught us about writing: Play with it. Don't be afraid to put words on the page. Digital storytelling allows kids to play, but it also teaches them to be meaningful in that play.

As soon as Harrison was done writing his story, he was *done with his story*. I wonder how the story might have taken shape if he had added pictures, video, or sound. I can imagine Harrison's skateboarding experience as a digital story. He would have engaged in all of the sophisticated thinking necessary to build such a story. His thinking would not have stopped once he delivered it to my e-mail inbox.

A couple of years ago, Al Stuart—the technology education teacher at the middle school where I teach—and I decided to collaborate on the idea of letting kids make animated cartoons from personal narratives they had written in my class. Here's how complex the collaboration was:

AL: I'll order twenty-two copies of a program called Frames.

ME: I'll ask my teammates if I can remove twenty-two kids from their regular classes for an entire day, and then I'll rewrite the remaining schedules for the week.

AL: Do you know anything about digital storytelling?

ME: Not a thing. Do you?

AL: No. Let's try it.

Of course the kids had already done so much of what Lisa Miller explains they need to do in this book—develop story ideas from questions they want to answer, construct storyboards that organize their ideas with compelling beginnings and surprising endings, and understand that the best stories have a hook that appeals to an audience as well as to the writer.

We sat the students down at computers and gave them six hours to tell their stories digitally. We found that none of them wanted to leave the computers—they were totally engaged and engrossed in all they could learn and produce. Adolescents, and even younger kids, do not need to move every seven minutes, as some "experts" insist, as long as they are genuinely interested in what they are creating (especially when using the tools that are so natural to them).

Lisa Miller shows us exactly how we can teach Harrison, or any student, to "make me a story." *Making* should be a key practice in all of our classrooms. Our students are already using technology. It is our job to help them *make meaning* with that technology.

What I love about this book is that Lisa alleviates a lot of our fears by showing us *one* aspect of technology: digital storytelling. She demystifies the process of incorporating technologies into our classrooms by letting us concentrate on the one thing that all of our students are good at—telling stories—and then shows us how to take this natural ability and turn it into what makes us literate in this century: the ability to think and learn and express ourselves through our words, our chosen images, and our actual voices. Like Don Murray, she is teaching us how to play, but how to play meaningfully. Throughout the book I am reminded that Lisa does far more than teach digital stories. She teaches us how to teach writing. Digital technology is the tool that makes the stories come alive.

Several years ago I was working with Hunter, Harrison's older brother, as he struggled with a piece of writing in the third grade. He told me he didn't like writing.

"Why?" I asked.

"Because, because . . . it's so quiet," he replied. "You have to do it by yourself, and then it just sits on the paper."

Through digital storytelling, Lisa shows us how to help our students bring their writing alive, to a place where their images and voices come bounding off the page. This is thrilling work for kids. And still the kids have to do the work of a good writer—they have to find a story that "answers some question that drives the writing forward" in a way that is appealing to themselves and to an audience. Lisa shows that, by weaving together writing and digital storytelling, we teach our students the strengths of both as they maneuver back and forth in an organized, strategic way to tell their stories.

This is complex work. In the process of crafting a digital story, students must constantly consider and reconsider ideas, organize information, synthesize, analyze, synchronize, evaluate, and assess. It is a recursive process that involves decisions about point of view, beginnings, endings, choice of words and images, voice and tone, mood, purpose, and audience. Lisa guides us meticulously through all of it. She shows us that our students have to solve real problems by complicating, yet enriching, their ideas as writers and storytellers. Through the digital stories the kids create, we see how sophisticated and genuine the process is, and how rewarding the results can be.

Among the many things I learned from Don Graves, professor emeritus at the University of New Hampshire, one of the most important concepts was that we should be teaching deeper, not wider. Lisa takes us deep into digital storytelling. What I realized as I read this book is that we teach students so much more when we concentrate on one thing to teach them well, instead of jumping from project to project or topic to topic without ever giving them time to really develop and apply their ideas and understandings. In *Make Me a Story,* Lisa invites, encourages, and instructs us to teach one thing—digital storytelling—deeply and thoroughly.

Students get to participate in a complex process that Lisa makes accessible, practical, and joyful. By relating her classroom experiences, she guides us through the ways we can teach our students to think, talk, write, and craft stories that are meaningful to them in a way that will make them meaningful to others as well.

We are in a different place with writing than we were just twenty years ago. The writing itself has not changed—it still needs to make us think, or feel, or learn something. However, the tools with which it is crafted and delivered to others have changed drastically. The students I teach in eighth grade were born into this digital age. They have played with technology their entire lives. They cannot believe that anyone who is still living today was alive before television was invented. (That would be me.) I have to find ways to help them compose their writing, interview others, write book reviews or trailers, and read others' writing using technology—either the school's or their own. If we don't have the tools of technology in our classrooms, we have to find ways to use the tools students carry with them.

Make Me a Story is for all teachers at all grade levels. Lisa teaches us the process of real writing for real reasons for a real audience using twenty-first-century technologies. We have to listen to the stories and learn all about the tools that bring those stories to life.

For years I have wanted to take Lisa's digital storytelling course at the University of New Hampshire, but our schedules have always conflicted. Don Murray often used to say to me, "You have to meet Lisa Miller. You have so much to learn from each other." From this book I have learned how to really teach digital storytelling. From this book I have also learned what Lisa has learned from the students with whom she has worked—how to listen for stories, how to teach writing, how to quietly wait to be surprised. Don Murray would be so pleased that we have finally *met*.

Linda Rief is an eighth-grade teacher at Oyster River Middle School in Durham, New Hampshire. She is an adjunct instructor in the University of New Hampshire's Summer Literacy Institute. She is the author or editor of numerous books, including *Inside the Writer's–Reader's Notebook, Vision and Voice, Seeking Diversity,* and *Adolescent Literacy* (Eds. Beers, Probst, and Rief)—all of which are Heinemann publications—and *100 Quickwrites* (Scholastic). She has participated in her first Webinar and learned to take pictures on her cell phone (just don't ask her how to get them off of there) but is not yet willing to give up her overhead projector.

Acknowledgments

I owe great thanks to all the students who shared their digital stories with me, and to all the fantastic, dedicated teachers who shared their time and their teaching expertise with me and helped me gather student stories, especially Ellie Papazoglou, Susan Carter, technology coordinator Jimi Emery, Debbie Finch, Julia Masury, Deanne Mayne (thanks for sharing your computer expertise too), librarian Janice Mudgett, and Michael Pelletier.

Thank you to all the teachers who took my summer digital storytelling classes at the University of New Hampshire. I learned so much from you. Special thanks to the 2009 class members, who helped me with this manuscript.

There would be no book without my colleagues Tom Newkirk and Louise Wrobleski, who encouraged me all through the process and have taught me so much about teaching; or without my mother, Carol Miller, who has always inspired me. Thanks to the Rag Bag Girls too, for your loving support. And I am lucky enough to belong to a Great Books reading group, whose members enthusiastically listened to me babble on about this book whenever I needed to. Thanks, everyone.

Thanks as well to my many journalism students at UNH who, as per my request, asked me now and then, "How's the book coming?" to spur me on, and who actually listened carefully to my answers. I was blessed with an amazing editor, Toby Gordon, and I thank her for all of her wonderful advice, encouragement, and wisdom. I also thank Chris Downey and Jay Kilburn, production; Rebecca Eaton, Chuck Lerch, Nate Butler, Zsofia McMullin, and Dan Tobin, marketing; Chandra Lowe, for her painstaking work on permissions; and copyeditor Nancy Sheridan, for her careful reading of the book and her excellent suggestions.

I also want to thank Linda Rief for the thoughtful and generous foreword.

The spirit of Don Murray was with me all the way.

Introduction

I first encountered the writing process at the University of New Hampshire while doing my master's degree work there. Having received a teaching assistantship, I was assigned to teach a section of freshman English and was told to use Don Murray's book *Write to Learn* (1987).

The book astonished me. I was a writer. I'd worked at a newspaper as a writer and editor for several years. I'd been an undergraduate English major and had written lots of papers. Sometimes I struggled with writing, and often, when it went well, I didn't know why, so I couldn't recreate the experience later. Yet here was a book that explained writing as a logical series of steps I could try and improve on. Here was a way to create a draft without agonizing first over what I would say. Here was a book that told me to trust my instincts and just write, seeking to be surprised by what showed up on the page.

I've been following Don's process model ever since and advocating it in classes I teach at the university. But I didn't begin to see how well the writing process and digital storytelling fit together until I helped create digital stories with a group of second graders in Portsmouth, New Hampshire. I was enchanted by their tales of lost princesses, mad professors, and trapped zoo creatures.

Their teachers led them through a process: brainstorming to decide what story to tell and how; drafting; and revising as they went along. Each student handwrote his or her story and created a book with four or five illustrations and an illustrated cover. The writing that went with each illustration was taped to each page. As they worked on the stories, I wandered around, asking questions about the characters and, if a student seemed stuck, what might happen to a certain character or how the story was going to end or what made the student want to write about this particular character in the first place.

When the writing and illustrations were finished, I took pictures with my digital camera of the front cover and inside pages of each student's book. Using a digital recorder, I then recorded each student reading his or her story. The students were thrilled to be hearing their own voices reading their own words. I was working with proud and happy writers.

After the recording, I imported the pictures and the audio into Microsoft PowerPoint. Then I sent copies of the completed stories back to the school.

I was amazed by how invested many of those students had become in writing the stories and recording the narration. I loved the stories. I wanted to see and hear more.

Since then, I've worked with many other elementary school teachers and students on digital storytelling. I've found that the writing process and digital storytelling go together naturally. Just as writing can be a process of discovery, so can digital storytelling, where images, words, and music all work together to create meaning. Even though visuals—photographs or pictures students have drawn or painted—are important elements of a digital story, writing a script for the story is the most important part of the process. It's through the writing that a student discovers what story he or she actually wants to tell and thinks through how the words will go with the images.

Digital storytelling and the writing process are powerful teaching tools. Through these digital projects students learn how to write good stories, how to make art and text work together, and how to use technology in creative ways. They also have a great time with the writing and storytelling and moviemaking all rolled into one project.

Don't be afraid of the technology. I'm not a computer expert. In fact, I was terrified the first time I taught with computers at UNH. I was going to offer a freshman English writing course in a computer lab for the first time and was agonizing over how I was going to do it. A wise colleague told me to remember that I already knew how to teach writing and the computers were just another tool to add to those I usually gave my students. I made it through that class, and ever since I've been trying out new technology in classes and learning to use it along with my students (who learn much more quickly than I do).

If I can teach digital storytelling, you can. Moreover, after you read this book, I hope you will want to.

Chapter
ONE

Stories That Matter

This was the transformation! The shift from reluctance to stamina—stretches of sustained writing. These students were writing and writing. The photos provided the visual support they needed to determine what was important in their story. The stories were important to them. They mattered.

—Ellie Papazoglou, New Hampshire reading specialist, working with
a third-grade class on digital stories

What does a family dog do when he's hungry and no one's around to feed him? (He raids the neighbor's cat food supply.) Why is the addax, an antelope, uniquely suited to living in the Sahara Desert? (This animal doesn't need to drink water; it gets the moisture it needs from the plants it eats.) How does an apple feel about being made into applesauce? (Not happy.)

Three elementary school students explored these questions through writing and technology. They all wrote scripts and gathered photographs to go with their words. With these, they created wonderful digital stories.

Josh's story about his pet opens with a picture of a black dog straining at his leash and some soft pop music in the background. A voice says, "Hi there, I'm Logan, and I love food. So now, about my people . . ." (see "Josh Logan" on CD). Janki's story starts with jazz and a panoramic view of the Sahara Desert, and she tells us that the desert, where the addax lives, is "a sandy and stony place" and the largest desert in the world. Sarah's story (see "Sarah and Apple" on CD) begins with a photograph of a girl, spoon in her mouth, eyes merry. Bouncy music plays in the background, and then a narrator says, "Hi, my name is Sarah, and this is how my mom and I make delicious applesauce." The photograph changes to one of an apple; the music becomes more frantic. This time a gruff voice says, "Hello, my name is Mr. Apple, and there is something I would really like to tell you. It is the story of being cooked in a fifty-foot pot so that we could be eaten up one by one."

Digital storytelling such as this involves using computers and software to marry text with art—often still photographs, drawings, or paintings but also video—as well as narration and music. Over the past three years, as I've worked with teachers and students in grades 1–5 to create these kinds of stories, I've learned this type of storytelling can teach writing and reading skills, motivate reluctant students, and help prepare youngsters for the digital sea many of them already swim in. I've seen magic happen.

I've helped students gleefully experiment with software; I've seen reluctant writers grinning as their digital stories were shown to classmates and visitors; I've observed students working intently (sometimes skipping lunch!) through the writing process to complete their projects. I've watched students view their own stories with pride.

How is digital storytelling *writing*? When you take students through the process of creating a digital story, you're taking them through the writing process. In fact, writing is paramount. The computer allows you to throw in lots of bells and whistles. But if authors of digital stories don't do the writing, don't take the time to draft and revise their scripts, then they don't get to the deep thinking we all need to do to tell the best stories. Teaching digital storytelling, you are still going to talk about audience, context, specific details, beginnings and endings, and everything else you talk about when you talk about writing. What you have to do is stretch the process a bit to include the visual and audio elements students will add to the writing.

What Do We Mean by *Story?*

Digital stories sometimes do tell what we traditionally think of as stories, as when students write about personal experiences or make up stories about superheroes or aliens from another planet or adventuresome pets. But digital stories may also tell about a historical or current event or explain a mathematical or scientific concept. They can be serious or funny, fiction or nonfiction, poetry or prose. The key for a successful digital story is that, rather than simply reporting the facts, it answers some question that drives the story forward, whether that question is, How do we use fractions in everyday life? (you can find the digital story "A Day with Fractions" on the Apple Learning Interchange—iLife in the Classroom Web site, http://edcommunity.apple.com/ali/collection.php?collectionID=7) or, What happens when three elephants decide they want wings? or, What was the battle of Antietam like for a young soldier facing the enemy for the first time? ("A Young Man's First Battle," on the Digitales Web site, http://www.digitales.us).

Why Teach Digital Storytelling?

Some of the students I've worked with had never created digital stories before I showed up at their schools. We went through parts of the process together. Through their personal narratives I learned about a hamster named Lucy who is an intrepid explorer, a dog named Moxie who catches frogs by a pond, and a bearded dragon named Leo. I learned how it feels to wear a first baseman's glove, what it's like to be coached by your dad in hockey, and what you see when you walk by a spooky deserted house. These student writers demonstrated why elementary schoolteachers should teach digital storytelling.

1. **Digital storytelling engages and empowers reluctant readers and writers and different types of learners. It makes everyone want to write.** Most students, if not all, were seriously invested in the writing of these stories. Students who ordinarily didn't put a lot of effort into their work did so. They wrote and wrote and wrote. Students who were already strong writers got a chance to try new skills and stretch themselves, since they had to match their words with illustrations and music and write scripts meant to be read aloud. Visual learners had illustrations to help them in building their stories. Some students revised all the way through the process to when we were recording their narration. "I don't like the way that sounds," one would say, rewriting a line and then rerecording. Students wanted to be sure to get these stories right, and not necessarily in the way I thought of as right, with the audio recorded without any mistakes or "uhs." They wanted their stories to sound like them, sometimes "uhs" and all, and to unfold the way they had envisioned. They were in charge of these stories.

2. **Digital storytelling projects can change how students see themselves and their classmates and can build community in the classroom.** Students who are not strong writers but are adept at working with computers gain confidence from this part of the process. Struggling readers find these stories manageable because the scripts are short, ranging from a couple of paragraphs or a few lines of a poem to a page and a half of prose. Working on these projects, some students see themselves as writers for the first time. Students become experts on the subjects of their stories and have the chance to read their own words in their own voices—a very powerful experience.

3. **Thinking about audience is an important part of the process.** Students I've worked with had a strong sense of audience right from the start of their digital storytelling projects and wanted to be sure the stories

would be viewed once they were completed. "Can I get a CD of this so my mom can see it?" "Can I show it to my teacher?" After I finished recording the voice-over for one third grader's story and we watched the completed story all the way through, he immediately jumped from his seat and asked if his story would be on YouTube. I explained that it wouldn't but that we were going to make sure he had a copy on CD to show his family. Students don't always have that sense of audience with a piece of writing, nor do students often excitedly cluster around one child's desk to read his or her latest essay. But from the start these digital stories were put together to be seen by others. The authors loved watching their stories with a live and appreciative audience (appreciative in part because the audience members had also done the project and knew what it took). Personal narratives were particularly heartfelt; students were very brave in telling those stories.

4. **Digital storytelling projects do not have to be complicated to be effective.** Many students' stories were three minutes long or shorter, including only four or five pieces of art. Nonetheless, students got a great deal out of creating the stories. As Ellie Papazoglou said of her group of third graders, "To me it seemed that this assignment opened so many doors to them for creating and composing a story. They could be creative; they told their own story; they had visuals to scaffold the development of their story. It was more than just writing, revising, and editing. This was a tool that provided some good support for composing a story, yet at the same time allowed for innovation and creativity" (2009).

5. **Stories can be done across the curriculum.** Many students write about personal experiences, but digital stories can be told about many subjects. (See Resource Box: Across the Curriculum for a Web site that offers ideas about possible digital storytelling subjects.) For example, elementary school students I've worked with or whose stories I've found on the Web have tackled subjects such as patriotism in the aftermath of September 11; heroes; three little fish outwitting a shark (a fairy tale); why students should have the opportunity to take art classes; onomatopoeia; biomes; and famous people in New Hampshire history.

RESOURCE BOX: ACROSS THE CURRICULUM

Meg Ormiston, coauthor (with Mark Standley) of *Digital Storytelling with PowerPoint*, offers good digital storytelling resources on her TechTeachers Web site (http://techteachers.com), including ideas for digital stories students can do in different subject areas. At the site, go to Resources, which brings you to the Digital Filing Cabinet, then to the link for Digital Storytelling, then to Ideas for Digital Stories Across the Curriculum.

6. **The process is the point; digital storytelling projects teach writing and technology skills.** Throughout the projects, students practice all sorts of important skills: using appropriate and interesting vocabulary; gathering and organizing information; showing and telling; analyzing the information (textual and visual) they're working with; explaining their stories for an audience; creating and presenting something original; and applying what they know about computers, technology, and storytelling to a new project. They learn about and try out the writing process, getting especially involved in revising, something students don't always want to do. They experiment with different storytelling structures. While working on digital stories, they think through how best to tell *and* show the stories, how the visuals work with the written text.

7. **The process draws on what students already know about storytelling—and moviemaking.** Students I worked with knew a lot about the conventions of telling a story both from books they'd encountered and from movies and TV. They had a sophisticated knowledge about visual elements that can make a story effective. They couldn't necessarily explain to me that they were panning across a picture or slowing the pace of a part of the story with slow music. But they knew that's what they were doing

and why. These students didn't choose words or pictures or music or effects randomly; they did them with intention. Almost every student wanted to tell me about some element of his or her story that had been carefully thought out. One youngster spent a long time deciding what anecdotes to share about the horses she cared for and how to match music to the horses' personalities—one shy, one a show-off. Another student, writing about his baseball team, thought hard about the photographs he had to work with and whether to put himself or his best friend first in the story (he went with his best friend). Some students used foreshadowing and carefully chosen transitions in their narrations. They wrote beginnings meant to grab viewers' attention and endings meant to satisfy viewers. They tried out different points of view and so were reminded that not everyone sees everything in the same way.

What's in This Book

This book will show you how to teach your students digital storytelling. It will explore the writing process and the technology, step by step. If you are nervous about using computers, you'll find this book easy to use.

I'll discuss different types of stories, what students gain from going through the writing process, and ways to assess such assignments, as well as how digital storytelling projects encompass skills prescribed by national education and technology standards. Along the way, I'll describe various student projects. The CD that accompanies this book features examples of students' digital stories.

My aim is to answer these questions: What elements make up a digital story? How do students work through the writing process to create digital stories? What sort of learning takes place?

The Technology: Software and Hardware

The program I'm going to take you through for creating digital stories is a free one called Microsoft Photo Story 3 for Windows, and many schools use it. It can be downloaded for free from the Microsoft Web site (http://www.microsoft.com) onto your school's computer system; the specifications for the program can be found on the Web site. It's only for PCs. There are other programs, including Microsoft Movie Maker, which is available on PCs, and iMovie, available on Macintosh computers. There are also programs you can purchase, including Adobe Premiere Pro and HD Final Cut Pro.

These other programs allow students to do more kinds of editing and create more visual effects than Photo Story 3; they also allow you to use video. Photo Story 3 does not. And the other programs give you more freedom in the way you use recorded voice-overs. In Photo Story 3, students must record each piece of the story individually, tied to the photograph or picture that piece of the story goes with, rather than recording the entire narrative and then adding it to the photographs.

But Photo Story 3 is simple, very easy to work with, and very easy to teach, so students don't get hung up for too long figuring out new software or messing with hundreds of different things a program can do. If you've never done digital storytelling before or have a large group of students to teach the software to, I recommend Photo Story 3. At each different step for creating a digital story, the program offers specific Help screens and can be learned quickly. One class I worked with started putting their digital stories together after a fifteen-minute demonstration by me.

What else do you need? You and your students can create great digital stories with a computer, a digital camera, and a computer microphone. You can use the digital camera to take photographs of students' artwork or have them take photographs, then download the photos into the computer. If you have a scanner, you can scan in photographs or images.

You can buy fancy sound equipment, but it's not necessary. The quality of sound you get with a microphone is just fine.

Preparing Students for Their Future

There is one more reason to teach digital storytelling. If we are going to give students all the skills they need to be successful in this world immersed in technology, we can't afford *not* to teach it—even at the elementary school level. In the future, more and more jobs are going to require the ability to use video-editing, image-editing, and sound-editing software, as more content is put onto the World Wide Web. Advertising, public relations, teaching, high technology, jobs we can't even imagine yet—all are going to require strong computer and storytelling skills. Right now, my journalism students absolutely must learn to put images and words together to tell stories online or they won't be prepared to report and write for news organizations.

Project Tomorrow, a national education nonprofit group in California, published a report in 2005, titled *Our Voices, Our Future: Student and Teacher Views on Science, Technology and Education*. After conducting a nationwide survey of students and teachers, the group reported that 73 percent of K–3 students and 94 percent of students in grades 3–6 use computers in their free time. Shouldn't we make sure they are also using them in school to do meaningful work?

Our students need to learn digital storytelling. They are inundated every day with information from TV and the Internet. We must help them sort through all of this information to find what they need to know and what they can use. Working on digital stories, they can begin to consider the impact of what they see and read and hear. Knowing how they've used their own words and images, they can better understand how others do so. Researching stories online, they can start to figure out what is reliable data and what is not. Creating stories, they can become active learners instead of passive receivers of information.

I'm not going to tell you that all writing projects should be turned into digital stories or that digital storytelling will win over every reluctant student or make every student a skilled writer. It is one more tool—a great tool—to add to our teaching toolbox. We can help students turn their words into stories they can see and hear. We can make sure they know they have stories to tell that matter.

How Do Writers Tell (Digital) Stories?

Question: Do you imagine the pictures or images in your head before you write, or do you have to draw them?

Answer: I imagine them very clearly and then attempt to describe what I can see. Sometimes I draw them for my own amusement!

—J. K. Rowling, Interview

How do the best writers tell stories that grab readers and hold their attention right to the end? That question is just as important when students are working on digital stories as it is when they are doing other writing assignments. It's true that the written text is only one element of several that make up a digital story. But the words students write, their digital storytelling scripts, are the foundations for these stories and provide the threads that connect the images. The images add to the text. That's why the writing matters and why you can approach the writing of digital stories in pretty much the same way you approach other writing assignments.

You may want to start by reminding students about what they have already learned about how writers tell great stories. Ask students questions to get them thinking about stories they like: What makes a story a good one? What makes you want to keep reading? What sorts of details do you remember best after you read a story? When writers tell stories about their own lives, what details do they choose to include and what kinds of things do they leave out? How do writers make factual information meaningful? How do writers connect the different parts of their stories? Where do they start their stories? Why do they end them the way they do?

Writers for any media, of fiction or nonfiction, choose specific details that matter for the stories they are trying to tell. They begin stories with interesting information and make you want to know more. They often have a central idea about the subject of their story that they want to get across. They present the story from a certain point of view and make clear transitions between different parts of their story. They write an ending that is satisfying, that feels like an ending. They explain why factual information matters, what it means to readers. Sometimes writers put us right in the middle of the action during part of the story.

Students should consider some or all of these possibilities when they put together digital stories, just as they would consider them when completing other writing assignments. With some students you might also talk about metaphors and similes or foreshadowing. One third grader I worked with told a story about his dog and began it by mentioning that things were crazier after the puppies came. I said, "Puppies? What puppies?" He said he was going to get to the puppies later in the story. He was foreshadowing what was to come.

Talking about books they've read will give students ideas about what they might write about and how, all the way through the writing process. We can all learn by imitating great writing, even though we eventually want to find our own writing style.

· ·

Elements of a Digital Story

In addition to discussing what goes into a good written story, you may want to discuss storytelling elements many digital stories have in common. The Center for Digital Storytelling (CDS) in California (http://www.storycenter.org), a nonprofit arts and education organization that offers digital storytelling workshops all over the world, has in the past listed these: point of view, dramatic question, emotional content, the gift of your voice, the power of the soundtrack, economy, and pacing. This list has been adopted by many; I followed it when I put my first digital story together during a CDS workshop.

(Note that the Center has since changed how it teaches workshops. Instead of talking about digital storytelling elements, it now cites Seven Steps of Digital Storytelling: owning your insights, owning your emotions, finding the moment, seeing your story, hearing your story, assembling your story, and sharing your story. You can find more information about these steps in the Center's Digital Storytelling Cookbook, http://www.storycenter.org/resources.html.)

I've adapted the Center's list somewhat for our youngest storytellers. Emotional content may not be appropriate for some assignments students are asked to do, though these assignments can work as digital stories. A "dramatic question" can be construed to mean something involving emotion at one extreme end of the emotional spectrum or the other. And I see pacing as something that comes from the way students read their stories, the music they choose for their sound tracks, and the transitions they use between the art they choose. So my list of elements includes the following:

- An interesting question to answer
- Impact
- A clear point of view
- Economy
- The power of a student's voice
- Art that helps tell the story
- The sound track

The first four can be elements of many kinds of writing students do; the last three are particular to digital stories. Naturally you can tailor any discussion about any of these elements to your students.

Digital stories do not have to include every element. I've seen interesting stories with only art and voice, or without voice-over but with slides featuring text incorporated into the stories. What your students include may depend on their ability level and the time they have to complete their stories.

It may take seven or eight class periods, fifty minutes each, to finish digital stories, but the project will take more or less time depending on how quickly the writing gets done, how complicated the stories are, how often your students have access to computers, and whether you have help or must record each student's narration yourself. Get parents or other volunteers to come in and help if you can. The more adults working with students and computers, the better.

Of course, some students will be more proficient in working with these elements and creating digital stories than others. Some stories will be more complicated or deep or polished than others. That's fine. Students will get a lot out of creating the stories no matter what the final products look like.

Showing Examples of Digital Stories

You probably discuss and model different types of writing for your students—personal narratives, fairy tales, fables, science reports—and so may want to show students some examples of digital stories before they begin their own. (See this book's accompanying CD for examples and Resource Box: Online Examples of Digital Storytelling for information on finding stories online.) You might get your students to create a list of what makes a great digital story by asking them to think about what makes the stories work, remembering that the list will include criteria they've discussed before about good writing: What do they like about a particular digital story? What do they not like? Is the story interesting? Are there any surprises in the story? Does the beginning grab their attention? Does the ending fit the story? Are there any questions the writer doesn't answer in the story but should? Does the writer include all seven elements?

Do they help tell the story? Is the story clear? Do the art and the text go together well? Does the story have a central idea or theme or message?

The Elements of Three Students' Stories

One story begins with a photograph of a massive tornado (see "Colby" on CD). The music we hear is fast, the notes tumbling along. The story's author, fourth-grader Colby, begins by telling us, "Tornadoes are very dangerous in this part of the world. One of the highest windspeeds for a tornado is more than 300 miles per hour." More dramatic tornado photos follow.

Another story begins with a photograph of the woodworking shop belonging to a young author's dad (see "Tyler Woodshop" on CD). We hear light rock music, and then the first photograph fades into a second, a close-up of some sort of machine. Slowly our view changes as the frame of the picture zooms out until we can see the whole machine, and we hear the author and narrator, third-grader Tyler say, "Swish, smash, oh great! Now who's paying for that? A board just slingshotted off the table saw and made a hole in the wall. I don't think we're getting that fixed because it will just happen again. Be careful. The table saw *can* be dangerous."

A third story opens with a photograph of a hamster in some tall grass (see "Sam Lucy" on CD). It's a wide shot—we can see how small the hamster is—that steadily zooms in until we see only the hamster. Over soft, happy music the storyteller, third-grader Sam, says, "Squeak, squeak. Hi, my name is Lucy. I'm a real explorer. I love to explore. I want to show you a time I had an exploring experience. It was at a weird, cool, and pretty place. There were a lot of things that were bigger than me, and some things that were smaller than me."

These three stories immediately draw listeners in and go on to make good use of the elements of a digital story. Let's see how.

An Interesting Question to Answer

Stories that answer interesting questions will invite readers in and keep them engaged to the end. The questions don't have to be complicated, but they've got to be answered by more than yes or no, or there's no tension or sense of discovery that drives the story, no surprise in store.

Colby's story answers the question, Why should we fear tornadoes? She sets up tension at the very beginning of the story when she tells us of the power of tornadoes. We want to know more.

Tyler started out knowing he wanted to write about his dad's woodworking shop, and as he wrote and put together his story, he began to see it as sort of a tour of the shop, highlighting the most interesting and important machines in the place. His story answers the question, What do the machines in the woodworking shop do and how does a person handle them? or even, Why do people need all of the machines in the woodworking shop?

Sam wanted to tell a story of Lucy, his hamster, out in the world. His question is, What does the outside world look like to a little hamster who goes exploring?

I do not think these students necessarily had these questions in mind when they started writing their stories, and maybe they didn't even realize they answered these questions. But they did find ways to tell their stories that took them beyond mere recitation of facts and so made the stories intriguing.

Impact

The best digital stories have an impact on the audience, whether they make people laugh or cry or teach them something amazing or important. If students consider impact when working on their stories—along with an interesting question—their stories will always be more than mere reporting of facts.

Colby's story is meant to teach us about tornadoes, and it's clear from the pictures she chose and the tone of her voice narrating that she wants us to take them seriously.

Tyler's story is also meant to teach us, about the woodworking shop. But his story is moving as well as informative; as you watch his story you come to realize how proud he is of his dad. He actually turns his story into an advertisement for his dad's shop.

And Sam's story makes us laugh and imagine what life is like when you're only a few inches tall.

A Clear Point of View

Digital stories give students a chance to try out different points of view—which can be great fun—and consider which one might help tell the story best. Students might, for example, write the story as though they were the animal or object the story is about, as Sam did and as third-grader Sarah did when she wrote about a day in the life of an apple from the point of view of the apple (see "Sarah and Apple" on CD); they might do the story in first person themselves, telling what they've seen and/or what they've learned; they might use a third-person narrator to describe the habitat of the common tree shrew or a road race between aliens from Mars and aliens from the Moon. They might see everyday things as really big or really small—like Lucy the hamster—or try to tell a story from the viewpoint of a friend or sibling. Colby's research makes her knowledgeable about tornadoes, and she tells the story as the researcher she is, relating what she's learned calmly, clearly, and confidently. Tyler is the expert when it comes to talking about the woodshop, so he's the appropriate narrator for that story. Sam, though, wants his viewers to see what things are like through Lucy's eyes—that's a main purpose of his story. Students writing digital stories must think about audience to make sure what they're trying to get across will be clear to others. How does a different viewpoint change the way a story is told? Does it change the way things should be described? Does it affect the details an author decides to include in the story?

Consider a book such as *The True Story of the Three Little Pigs!* "as told" by Jon Scieszka and illustrated by Lane Smith (1989), where the story is narrated by the wolf instead of the pigs (I use this book in my newswriting classes to get my students to think about point of view and about doing research that gets below the surface of a story). The facts of the story are changed some, but what is most unlike the usual version of the tale is the way the wolf's actions are interpreted. Trying out different points of view may get students to think about how differently the same incident or issue can be seen by different people, and why. It may also help them to think about whether they're getting the whole story when they read or hear something online or on television.

Economy

Digital stories are generally short, three to five minutes long. They're short for a couple of practical reasons: The computer files with images and audio can take up a lot of space on a computer server, and keeping them short makes them manageable for you and your students. But it's also true that a story that is short and therefore tightly focused on an experience or theme can be more compelling than a sprawling story about the same subject. If students want to tell longer stories about trips or other experiences they've had, encourage them to pick only parts of those trips or experiences to write about and to be choosy about what they include in the story. A digital story should have one central meaning, one central theme.

Economy applies to the words and sentences used too. Stories are most often in prose form but can be poems, and scripts may be as short as a few paragraphs or lines of a poem. You might get students to think about what they're writing as similar to a poem in the way few words are used to convey meaning, with nothing extraneous left in. They should think about choosing only the most interesting and/or important details for their story and try to use only a few sentences to go with each image, so they're getting rid of words that don't do any work, that don't move the story along.

Looking at picture books can also help students think about economy, if they consider what specific details writers include (and maybe what they don't) to tell their stories. The book *Song of the Water Boatman and other Pond Poems* (2005), by Joyce Sidman, includes short poems about pond life along with a paragraph per poem of true information about the subject of each poem (and beautiful illustrations by Beckie Prange). Students could consider what's included in both parts of the story about each living being—poem and paragraph—and talk about why the writer chose only those things to show or tell.

Colby simply shows us different views of tornadoes. The photos show us how menacing and destructive they are; she doesn't have to describe everything the photos show. She also economizes with her words, choosing telling details to include in her text such as how one tornado killed 695 people and damaged 15,000 homes. Her audience gets the message about how dangerous tornadoes are.

Tyler's story continues with photographs of the woodshop's machines and short explanations of what they do and, in a couple of cases, what trouble somebody can get into if he or she doesn't use the machines properly. He's chosen the information viewers most need to know and left out the rest. When a photograph of the edge bander comes up, he tells us, "The edge bander is a machine that heats up small balls of glue. It puts edges onto the boards. These boards are then used to make wood tables. One thing you should not do is pour the entire bag [of glue] because it would make a mess." That's definitely important to know!

Sam's story is told through five photographs. Each one shows Lucy in a different setting, and we're told about what she sees and feels and thinks as she explores. "Help, help, I'm being chased by a black snake," she tells us. "Oh, it's just a black pipe. Whoa! Look at that big hole right in front of me. I hope I don't fall in it. Wow, look at that bush right next to me and look at those purple flowers on the top of it." Sam's chosen the most vivid or surprising things in each picture to tell us about. In a brief but detailed story we're let in on what Lucy would most notice about the outdoors and what's most important to her. We also start to look at ordinary things around us in new ways.

The Power of a Student's Voice

A student's voice is one of the most compelling parts of a digital story. Reading their own stories empowers students. Hearing the stories in their own voices does the same. We listen eagerly to stories told out loud because *someone* is telling them. We love to hear (and read about) people talking. In my journalism classes, I tell students that sometimes the most compelling parts of a news story are direct quotes from sources, which allow those sources to speak directly to readers. Imagine the story of Little Red Riding Hood without the voices of the wolf and Red. The scene where she confronts the wolf might be written something like this: "Red Riding Hood looked at the figure in the bed and thought it had awfully big ears, eyes, and teeth. The wolf told her these were all so she could see, hear, and finally eat her." The story definitely loses something in this telling.

Instead, we usually have dialogue for this part of the story—two characters talking to each other: "Grandmother, what big eyes you have!" "The better to see you with, my dear." "What big ears you have!" "The better to hear you, my dear." "What big teeth you have!" "The better to eat you!" The drama is in the characters' own words.

You'll find when you do digital stories that some students have never heard their own voices recorded before. You might play other classmates' recordings before recording theirs, to put them at ease. This voice-over is a way for students to put their personal stamp on the story and present it to classmates and others without having to physically stand up in front of the class; it's a new way to present themselves and their work. The way students read their stories, emphasizing certain things and reading fast or slow—pacing—sets a tone or mood for the story too.

Students often say they don't like their voices when they hear them for the first time, but they still take pride in these self-narrated pieces. With Sam's, Tyler's, and Colby's projects, the voices of the narrators really make the stories come to life. The voices reach out to viewers, bringing them into the stories.

Many software programs, including the one I'm featuring in this book, Microsoft Photo Story 3 for Windows, allow you to use a microphone to record students' voices right into the program. (You'll find more on this in Chapter 4.)

Art That Helps Tell the Story

The main difference between digital stories and some of the other writing assignments your students do is that art is an important part of the telling of these stories. Your students may download photos or clip art from the Web (see Resource Box: Finding Images, Music, and Sound Online for sources); take photos with a digital camera and download them into the computer system or from a CD made of the photos if you use disposable cameras; or draw or paint their own illustrations to go with their stories. If you can have students take their own photographs or draw or paint pictures, do it. This strengthens the sense of ownership students feel when creating these stories.

RESOURCE BOX: FINDING IMAGES, MUSIC, AND SOUND ONLINE

Online sources for free photographs, art, and music include the following, which you can find by Googling the names or checking the Web sites listed in the "References and Resources" section at the end of the book:

- Classroom Clipart. Free images.

- Pics4Learning. As explained on the Web site, Pics4Learning is "a copyright-friendly image library for teachers and students. The Pics4Learning collection consists of thousands of images that have been donated by students, teachers, and amateur photographers. Unlike many Internet sites, permission has been granted for teachers and students to use all of the images donated to the Pics4Learning collection."

- The New York Public Library Digital Gallery. Offers images that can be downloaded free for classroom use and student projects.

- Discovery Education's Clip Art Gallery. Geared toward educators and students, with free material that is intended to be used for school projects, though there may be limits on how much you can download.

continued

- Kitzu. Offers free educational kits centered around subjects. The kits can include copyright-friendly photos, video, illustrations, music, and text.

You may also want to use Google's Image search, but keep in mind that the images it brings up may be copyrighted.

For music, try Soundzabound, which is a royalty-free music library (not free, though; schools must pay licensing fees to use the music) or Freeplay Music, which allows students to use music at no charge for educational projects (read the Terms of Use on the Web site carefully). Also check out FindSounds, a free site where you can search for sound effects.

Many digital storytelling sites offer links to art and music resources for teachers and students, such as the Digitales site created by Bernajean Porter. Keep in mind that any photo sites not specifically created for education may include images that are not appropriate for young children.

Downloading Images from the Web

If you're downloading images from the Web, you need to pay attention to the resolution of the image, measured in dpi, dots per inch. The more dots in every square inch of an image, the better the quality of the image when you import it into a computer program that enlarges it for showing on the computer screen. Bernajean Porter, on her Digitales Web site, recommends images with no less than 720x534 dpi for digital storytelling projects. Otherwise, your images will be blurry when shown as part of the story.

Also, before you download an image from the Web, click on the thumbnail version on the Web site to get the full-sized image. Then download that image onto your computer, not the small thumbnail version.

The number of images students use is up to you; effective stories can be told with only three or four images, and the most a three-minute digital story would include is fifteen or so. Limiting the number of images students use makes them concentrate on the story, and the story becomes the deciding factor in what images to use, not the other way around. It also makes the stories easier to complete in less time, so at least the first time you have students create digital stories, limit the number of images they can use to four or five. The art should do work; it should help show what the narration talks about and may even convey information not included in the narration that helps move the story along.

The children's picture books I most love aren't just beautiful to look at; the pictures truly help tell the story, the visuals and the text complement and complete each other. Look at *Owl Moon* by Jane Yolen (1987), illustrated by John Schoenherr. It's a story about a young girl and her father who go out in the winter night to search for owls. The illustrations are beautiful, the text is spare, and they work wonderfully together. There's one place where the child and father, dressed for the cold, stop in the middle of a clearing in the woods, beneath the moon. The picture, with its muted colors and many trees, seems to say "cold" and "night" and "mystery," and, because the picture shows the people so small in the landscape, it captures the way it feels to be in the woods on such a night looking for a wonderful creature that is not at your beck and call. The words of the book alone would not be enough, and neither would the pictures, but they each enhance the effect of the other. That's the way the best digital stories work too.

We say, "A picture is worth a thousand words." Sometimes that's true. But in an increasingly complicated world, where TV and the Web bring to our students lots of aural and visual and textual information, it matters that we teach them to make sense of what text and visuals do together, and how to tell stories using both.

Begin by having students consider how the illustrations in a book work with the text. Do the pictures show exactly what the writing does, or do they include things that aren't written down? Do the pictures go well with the writing? Are there places where the pictures tell part of the story better than the writing, or the writing better than the pictures? A book such as *A Couple of Boys Have the Best Week Ever* (2008), by Marla Frazee, about two boys going to nature camp, shows this well, because there are places where the pictures tell a slightly more accurate (and funny) story than the text does, and vice versa. For example, in one part of the story the boys are supposedly resting in "quiet meditation" after camp, but the illustration shows them furiously playing video games.

One second grader created a whimsical digital story about a little bear, Fluffy, who—though he doesn't mean to—keeps getting into trouble (see "Chris and Fluffy" on CD). Chris has a sequence of his own drawings that show things the text does not describe. For example, in one picture the bear, wearing a cape, tries to leap across the room without knocking anything over. The narrator says, "'Phew, that was close,' said Mom." The next picture shows Fluffy on the floor where he has fallen after leaping. The narrator says, "Mom asked, 'Are you OK?' 'No,' said Fluffy sadly." The narrator tells us later that the bear got in trouble again the next day but doesn't tell us how. Instead, the picture shows us: He was playing basketball and the ball ended up someplace it was not supposed to be.

Tyler and Sam were in a third-grade class where the teacher gave students digital cameras to take home and told them to take pictures of things that were important to them. For stories about three wishes, some first and second graders drew their own pictures of the people wishing, the fairy granting the wish, and the things the wishers received. One first grader painted beautiful pictures of penguins in the Andes for a story called "Penguins in Action" (see this story on CD). For other stories, students used clip art or photographs they downloaded from the Web.

Colby downloaded compelling photographs from the Web for her story. Tyler took photographs of the most interesting machines in the woodshop. Sam placed Lucy in settings where she'd find a lot to explore. Without the words, the pictures themselves would only tell part of the story; without the pictures, the stories would be flat. In all three cases, both elements work together to make for interesting storytelling.

I'm a big fan of original student artwork for digital stories. If they're taking photographs of their own, or drawing or painting illustrations rather than pulling art from the Web, students feel more like the stories belong to them, like they're in control. They also have the chance to really make the art work with the text. If you have them downloading art from the Web, they'll still think through that connection, though they may have a hard time getting art that shows exactly what they want it to. This is one reason you may want to have them create at least some illustrations themselves. When students pull images from Web sites, they may choose the same sort of image over and over, or images that don't quite match the text. I'm not saying your students can't do successful stories with images they get off the Web. I'm saying they may not get exactly what they're looking for—though that can mean they get quite creative in showing what happens in their story. For example, one third grader, another Sarah, tells a story her mom has recounted to her lots of times, about the day a little boy fell off of the school bus her mother was riding on when she was Sarah's age. Sarah uses clip art and photographs found online to illustrate her story, and when she gets to the part about the bus hitting a bump and the boy falling out, she shows a clip-art image of a bus tilted on its side, as if it's hit a big bump, then a photograph of a road, a long stretch of asphalt, to show us where the boy fell. It works.

If your students are working with artwork they find online, you'll want to talk with them about copyright issues. (See the information on copyright on page 28.)

The Sound Track

In digital stories, students can also set a certain mood and pace with the music, the sound track, they use. From movies, students know slow, somber music goes with a sad story and fast, energetic music with action. If you want to talk to students about the power of music, you might use movies as examples. Imagine the bicycle chase scene in *E. T.* when the boys' bikes suddenly lift into the air without the triumphant music playing in the background. The scene would lose so much of its intensity and joy without the music.

Photo Story 3 for Windows allows students to create original music, using options included in the program, to go with their stories as the last step in the process of creating those stories. They get to choose a genre, such as classical or country; a style, such as '80s rock; bands or instruments, such as orchestra or electric guitar; moods, including adventurous or sad; different tempos; and different intensities.

Colby used different music for each photograph in her story, and while that's a bit distracting, she chose music that's fast-paced and sometimes dissonant to hint at the tornadoes' speed and the chaos they cause. Tyler created music with fast beats for most of his pictures, giving the story some movement; Sam created music that sounded dramatic, also with a fast beat, adding a bit of tension to his story. Another student I worked with, whose story was about saying goodbye to his mentor, said he used sad music because the story was about a sad day.

Students can also import music they've found on the World Wide Web, but remember that some of these works—certainly music from an artist's CD—are copyrighted. Not all music Web sites offer music files free, and some sites require you to set up an account. Photo Story 3 will accept files in the following formats, meaning the files will have one of these suffixes at the end of the file name: *wma* (Windows Media Audio), *mp3*, or *WAV*. Usually you can choose the format when you download music from the Web. (For more information, see Resource Box: Finding Images, Music, and Sound Online on page 23.)

About Fair Use and Copyright

I'm not out to make you paranoid about copyright, but you should pay attention to fair-use guidelines, and your students should understand that they can't always simply download someone else's work and use it in their own projects. Too often these days students figure that because something is available on the Internet, they can use it and use it without crediting the source. The fair-use doctrine allows some use of copyrighted works for classroom instruction and other purposes. But there are guidelines as to how much material can be used, and credit must be given to those who created the copyrighted works.

Copyright and fair-use guidelines came into existence long before multimedia. But as explained in an article entitled "The Educator's Guide to Copyright and Fair Use," written by Linda Starr (2004) and posted on the *Education World* Web site, in 1996 the Consortium of College and University Media Centers (CCUMC) brought together publishers, educators, industry representatives, and legal experts "to draft a set of fair use guidelines for educators and students to use while creating multimedia projects that include copyrighted works. The guidelines they developed, although not legally binding, do represent an agreement among most institutions and organizations affected by educational multimedia. Following the guidelines should keep you and your students safe from charges of copyright infringement" (2004).

These guidelines, posted on the Web site of the Consortium of College and University Media Centers, state that "students may incorporate portions of lawfully acquired copyrighted works when producing their own educational multimedia projects for a specific course." There are limits to how much material can be used, though the guidelines exempt K–6 students from closely following those limits. You should, however, know what the limits are and have students follow them as much as possible. The limits, as set out in the *Education World* article, include these:

- Up to three minutes or 10 percent, whichever is less, of a single copyrighted motion media work

- Up to 30 seconds or 10 percent, whichever is less, of music and lyrics from a single musical work

- Up to five photographs or illustrations by one person and no more than 15 images or 10 percent, whichever is less, of the photographs or illustrations from a single published work (Starr 2004)

Young students don't have to know all the detailed ins and outs of these guidelines. They can understand, though, what it would feel like to have someone take pictures they painted or stories they wrote and claim them for his or her own. They should be taught to keep track of where they get all photographs or other elements they download from the Web and write up a works cited page to be included in or with the project.

As I've discussed previously, there are Web sites offering copyright-friendly or copyright-free materials for educators and students (see Resource Box: Finding Images, Music, and Sound Online on page 23). Of course, if students take their own photographs or create their own images and music for digital stories, you'll be home free.

Chapter
THREE

Taking Students Through the Writing Process: Part One

I have begun a voyage of discovery. The initial satisfaction from writing is surprise: we say what we do not expect to say in a way we do not expect to say it.

—Don Murray, *Write to Learn*

Learn to value the process, not the product.

—Jane Yolen, Interview

Surprises pop up all the way through the process of creating digital stories. Students are surprised by what they write, by how their art and text work together, by how their voices sound reciting their own words.

Students love putting the stories together with images and music on the computer, but before they get there, they must do the writing. Writing is thinking, so through writing they find out what they want to say and how they want to say it in the scripts. Even though the visuals are an important part of digital stories, this thinking/writing is what digital stories are built on. You'll want to take students through at least some parts of the writing process, the different steps writers go through to create stories. The process will help them see themselves as writers. It will help them get the writing done. And it will make the stories stronger than if students concentrated mostly on the images instead of on the writing.

There is no one process, no one way of talking about the steps writers follow. My friend and mentor Don Murray, who pioneered the writing process, revised his own models through eight editions of his book *Write to Learn*. In the seventh edition (2002), he listed the steps as these: focus, research, draft, revise, and edit; in the eighth edition (2005), he listed them this way: write before writing, research for writing, begin writing, keep writing, and finish writing. You can tailor the process to your students, whatever grade they're in, to help them be successful.

Although the texts for digital stories are short, students can still follow the steps of the writing process to create good scripts. In fact, the brevity of the scripts can be helpful; students may find such texts easier to work with and revise than longer ones.

As we grow as writers, we develop our own processes that work for us. But for young writers, a model such as Murray's provides a coherent way to talk about how students can get from an idea to a finished draft, and a way for thinking about writing in general that can serve these students well all through school and beyond. The writing process models show students that great writing isn't created by magic—that published writers' pieces don't suddenly appear perfect and whole on the page. Students learn there are steps they can follow, practice, and improve upon. If they run into roadblocks while writing, they can go back to one step and work on that step to solve the problems. The process also offers students ways to experiment and find out what writing techniques work best for them—and they can apply this experimentation to other writing projects they do. If they practice a process again and again, they'll always be able to get the writing done. And they'll make discoveries about what they have to say and about themselves as writers along the way. I've encountered students who, through the process, discovered what was most important to them about families or friendships or places they'd lived, or what most interested them about a subject they'd researched, like the child who wrote fiction about a polar bear but did factual research and then decided to focus on the polar bear's search for food.

Here are the writing process steps and the associated tasks I'll discuss in this chapter and the next:

Write before writing. Finding a subject; brainstorming, mapping, and other prewriting activities; asking questions about the subject.

Research for writing. Recollecting details about an experience; asking questions about a research subject; conducting research in the library and/or on the Internet; interviewing others; and collecting images.

Begin writing. Finding a focus; beginning a draft; considering point of view and audience; and planning the story, which includes thinking about images that might go with the story.

Keep writing. Developing a whole draft with a strong beginning and ending, transitions, concrete language, and interesting details; putting together the images; storyboarding to figure out what images will go with what text; and splitting the written script into pieces to go with the images.

Finish writing. Putting the story together in the computer, with images, transitions, voice-over narration, and music; revising as needed; and showing the stories to an audience.

This model implies that the process is linear, and of course it's not. A writer may focus and research, then go back and refocus, then move to drafting, then decide more research is necessary, and so on; students will revise through the drafting of scripts and up until they finish the stories. The model is simply an effective way to talk about writing and sets out ways for students to work through writing projects. It also offers students ways to experiment and find out what writing techniques work best for them.

Much of this—the collecting, focusing, and drafting—can be done (or at least started) in the classroom without computers, unless you want students to conduct research or find images on the World Wide Web, use computer clip art, or type up their scripts on computers. Once they've completed a draft of their text, collected their images, and created a plan for matching images with text, they'll be ready to work on the computers with a program such as Microsoft Photo Story 3 and begin putting all the elements together.

I've known first and second graders who, with some one-on-one help, have gone through part of the writing process and put their stories together on a computer, using Photo Story 3. I know that some of the youngest students won't be ready to go through all of these steps in depth or answer all of the questions I'm going to pose to help students through the writing process. You can pare down the model to the basics: find a subject, get the information and images you need, write the script, figure out what images go with what text, and put the text together with images using a computer. You can add any of the exercises, strategies, or questions I suggest if you think they will help your students through the process.

With first- and second-grade students you may want to concentrate mostly on finding a subject and on making the pictures and words go together. In fact, the first time you have students do digital stories, whatever the grade level, you may want to concentrate on focus—what main thing each student wants or needs to say—and making the pictures work with the words. When students do additional digital stories, you can have them consider other concerns, such as writing great beginnings and endings, or showing and telling.

You may decide to have students work together in pairs or groups on digital stories rather than having them do individual stories. For an online story about holidays (Digital Storytelling in the Scott County Schools Web site, http://www.dtc.scott.k12.ky.us/technology/digitalstorytelling/ds.html), first and second graders were split into teams. Each team dealt with one aspect of the story: images, music, scanning, cropping, or story. The digital story featured a different narrator for each holiday. Other examples of collaborative stories on the Web include one about the life cycle of the Granny Smith apple by a third-grade class (*Granny Smith*, Digitales Web site, http://www.digitales.us) and one about the battle of Antietam written and illustrated by three young authors (*A Young Man's First Battle*, Digitales Web site).

Sometimes teachers work with a class to create a group story: Students paint or draw one picture each, write a short poem or a paragraph to go with the picture, then turn it over to the teacher, who uses the material to create one digital story. A couple of teachers I worked with did this with their students' poems and drawings about nature. They still recorded each student reading his or her poem so that all of the students' voices were heard.

Even if students are doing individual stories, you might want them to work in pairs so they can help and support each other as they go through the writing process and work on the computers. The important thing is to make the projects workable for you and your students.

Before you have students create digital stories, you may want to do one of your own so you're comfortable with how the story and images go together. Teachers in digital storytelling classes I've taught have done personal narratives, introductions to books their students are going to read, and introductory lessons on subjects including clouds (to introduce students to the different kinds) and the making of a peanut butter and banana sandwich (to introduce students to the writing of how-to pieces).

· ·

Write Before Writing

Students first need to come up with subjects to write about and start to focus on what they want to say about those subjects. They do not have to know in advance what they want to say—they'll figure it out as they go. This also means they don't have to laboriously plan out what they're going to write beforehand, which some students wouldn't do anyway. They're going to discover the story and create the story as they write. I've seen some of my own college students agonize over starting stories, worrying about what the whole is going to say and wanting their beginnings to be perfect. If students follow a model of the writing process, they'll just plunge in and write, knowing they can go back and revise later.

Subjects for First Digital Stories

For their first digital stories you might give your students a topic to start with, as with one second-grade class whose assignment was to write about someone who wants something and has to overcome an obstacle to get it. You might have them write personal narratives, fables, fairy tales, or poems. Some students I met read a version of the old folktale about a couple and their three wishes and then wrote their own three-wishes stories. One third-grade teacher told me that during the school year (not just for digital storytelling projects) she has students write narratives about family members and about scary things that have happened. Students might tell stories about historical figures that grab their interest, or about the community they live in. They could explore a different country by pretending they live there, doing research and writing a first-person piece. They could study certain animals and write fiction or nonfiction that shows something about the animals' life and habits. They could write poems about colors or weather. If your class keeps interest journals—journals about different subjects that students take turns writing in—those might be the source of topics for digital stories. Almost any subject can be explored through a digital story. Can a student draw pictures (or take photographs, or find pictures) of what is featured in the story? If the answer is yes, he or she will be able to use them to put together a digital story.

Prewriting

To get students to choose an idea and focus on what they want to write, you may want them to do some prewriting. One way is to have them brainstorm ideas on a piece of paper—simply making a list of whatever comes into their heads that they might write about. For nonfiction pieces that students will need to research, you can have them brainstorm a list of what they already know about the subject, questions they'd like to be able to answer about that subject, or things they think their classmates (their audience) would like to know. Students can brainstorm in writing on their own or aloud as a whole group or in small groups or pairs to come up with subjects and story lines. No matter how they do it, they'll be starting to think about what their stories might be.

A brainstorming list for a story about the family dog might look like this:

tug-of-war

running through the yard

eats the neighbor's cat food

likes treats

walks

swimming in the lake

A brainstorming list for a story about animals that live in the Sahara Desert might look like this:

desert

hot

not much water

what can live there without water?

lots of sand—sandstorms?

Another form of brainstorming is mapping. Students write a subject or topic they want to consider in the center of a piece of paper, then draw lines from that main topic out to related things that come to mind. When they're done, the main subject is surrounded by lines that lead to other topics. This is a good method for students who are more comfortable visualizing images than writing lists. (See Figure 3.1.)

One more type of prewriting is freewriting. Here students write whatever comes into their heads, but unlike brainstorming, which results in a list, freewriting is a stream-of-consciousness narrative. Students simply write as they think, not worrying about spelling or grammar. A part of my freewrite for this chapter looks like this:

> *don't forget writing is paramount don't lose sight of the texxt that's what you need to remember and then also all of the rpewriting and focusing and other stuff you can do and what kind of music is there in writing also transitions and connectors examples fropm stories here? talk about transitions and connectors*

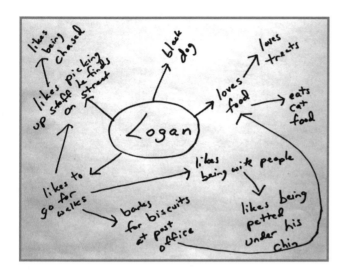

Figure 3.1 My rendition of a map using information about Josh's dog from the story "Josh Logan" (on CD)

It only makes sense to me, but that's OK, because it's just writing to build a real draft on.

With all of these prewriting techniques you have the students write or map very quickly, so that they aren't blocked by worrying if what they're coming up with is good or not. Don Murray used to say this was to outrun the internal censor we all have in our heads that tells us that what we just wrote was awful and we'd better try again. Listen to the censor and you'll never get any writing done. Just write.

Once students have done some brainstorming, mapping, or freewriting, they can look over what they've written to see if there are any words, phrases, or details that stand out to them that they'd really like to write about or include in a story. This may give students places to start.

You may want to model prewriting for your students. You could choose a topic for a personal narrative, such as your pet, or a topic you and your students have been exploring. Then try a quick brainstorming list, map, or freewrite on the board or on a computer hooked up to a projector.

You could also have students brainstorm as a group about some topic, with you writing down the list of details or information they'd want to include in a story, questions they might want the story to answer, or questions they'd need to research before writing the story.

Other Ways to Find Subjects: Lists and Questions

You could have students put together a list describing things they know about or know how to do, or have them brainstorm a list of family and friends if you want them to write about someone they know. If you show them other students' digital stories before they start, those will also give them ideas for their own.

As a journalist, I ask lots of questions, and I suggest that throughout the writing process you have students ask themselves questions: to find a subject, to find a focus, to figure out what to include in their story, and to consider whether they've said what they wanted to say. At this prewriting stage, if students are trying to find subjects to write about, they can ask themselves questions such as these: What makes me mad? What makes me happy? What makes me sad? (A group of first and second graders did stories about emotions in which they made statements such as, "I am the happiest when I get ice cream" [see "Katie" and "Calder" stories on CD].) What surprises me? What do I wonder about? What do I already know something about but would like to explore further? What is important to me? Who is important to me? What subject have I read about that I'd like to write about?

If students already have subjects or a specific assignment in mind, they might ask themselves questions to focus their topics. Why do I want to write about this? What do I most want to tell others about this? What makes me happy/mad/sad about this? What surprises me about this? What's the most important or interesting thing I can tell people about this subject? These questions can work whether students know a lot or only a little about their subject. If they don't know very much, the questions can show what sort of information they should be looking for.

You could model this activity too, or have the whole class try it with a topic they know or are going to be researching. Students could pair up and ask each other questions or simply talk about what they might like to write about.

I would have students actually write down the answers to the questions if possible so they can start to focus on what they want to include in their stories. But for the youngest students, just talking about the answers to some of these questions, in a group or pairs or with you, may work fine.

Pictures First?

Students can also begin with artwork instead of words. If they've already taken photographs or painted or drawn pictures before writing, they can brainstorm off of the images. They can ask themselves any of these questions: What's going on in this picture? Why is that happening? What happened right before or right after this picture? What's the most interesting thing about the picture? What do I like about this picture? What do I want to explain about this picture?

If you want students to practice this questioning first, show the class a photograph or illustration from a book and ask them some of the questions listed above. You might also ask whether the picture seems to be about something happy or something sad, and why they think that. These questions may help them figure out how much of a story pictures can tell and what then needs to be included in the text. It's also a way to get them thinking critically about what they see, useful thinking when surfing the Internet.

In Chapter 2 I mentioned students in a third-grade class who began their digital storytelling projects by taking digital photographs of things that were important to them. Pictures such as those can help students who struggle with writing, acting as a sort of outline, or what some educators call "scaffolding," to build the story on. The pictures can be starting points or reference points that help students write their scripts. Often, though, students go beyond what's in the pictures to include much more, everything they want us to know about their subject. As they go on in the writing process, the images may also help them figure out how to order things in the story, and even how to begin and end it.

For example, third-grader Lenny wrote a story about his dad (see "Lenny's Dad" on CD). He used four photographs, and his script is inspired by the content of the photographs. The first one is of his dad holding one of Lenny's siblings, and the narrator tells us, "This person right here is my dad. . . . My dad loves playing with me and my brothers." The next photo is of Lenny, his dad, and a girl, all with hockey sticks at the ready. The narrator says, "Oh, I didn't tell you my dad coaches me in hockey?" When that photo switches to one of his dad standing next to a truck, the narrator says, "This is my dad up close. You can see here the word *nurseries* [on the truck in the photo]. My dad loves his job very much as he loves me." Not all students who create digital stories about their parents include information about their jobs, but Lenny is so proud of his dad he suggests that viewers who want trees should contact his dad at the nursery where he works—and Lenny even offers the nursery phone number.

One third grader I worked with had seven pictures of dogs ready for his story, but no script. I started asking him questions: Do the dogs know one another? Do they have an adventure together? Do you want to tell us a little bit of information about each dog, showing how each is different from the others? He wasn't sure, but my questions gave him possible places to start. Sometimes a question such as, What happens in your story? is enough to get a student to start writing. If the student's answer is "I don't know," you might get the student to brainstorm or freewrite some more about what could happen, or to tell you why he or she wanted to write about this subject in the first place.

Whether students begin with their images or with their writing may depend on their ability level and the assignment you've given them. I've seen students work in both ways successfully. You should proceed in whatever order makes the writing easiest for your students. But even if they start with images, they must then go through the writing process. The writing must still carry the main thread of the story, with the art adding information to show what they're telling and maybe what they're not telling with words.

Research for Writing

Once they've got their subject, students can collect details or other information they want to use in their scripts and stories. If they're working on personal narratives, they can recollect the sensory details—sights, sounds, tastes, touches, smells—and the feelings and actions they remember and want to include in their stories. In Sarah's story about the apple being made into applesauce (see "Sarah and Apple" on CD), she offers some descriptive details about the cider mill where the apples come from: "This is the cider mill in Loudon, with the smell of fudge, doughnuts, and the smell of apple blossoms. Also there are jugs of chocolate, vanilla, and even strawberry milk."

Students can ask themselves, What do I remember? What did it look like, smell like, taste like, feel like, sound like? What happened? Students might answer these questions in writing, or verbally, working in pairs, or they can draw pictures to spark memories. Students might brainstorm or freewrite again to collect such details. They might interview family or friends about an experience, or talk out their stories with classmates. If students are paired up, one student can say what his topic is, and the other can tell him what she would like to know about that subject, what questions she would like the writer to answer.

If students are going to write about a topic outside their own personal experience, they can ask themselves, What do I already know, and what do I need to know? At this point, they may begin to research a subject on the Web or in the library. You may want to remind them that it's important that they keep track of where they get their information (and their images), whether it's from a book or the World Wide Web. That way they can create a Works Cited page and give credit to those whose information they use.

Questions About Images

This is also the point in the process where students may start to collect photographs or plan art for their stories if they haven't done this before beginning the writing process. Again, brainstorming or freewriting or talking out the story may help them figure out what images they need. They can ask themselves one basic question: What do I want to show my audience? Other questions can follow: Do I need to show the who or what or where of my story? Do I need to show what happened or is happening? Who is telling (narrating) my story and what would be important to him or her? What do I most want to show? Considering some of these questions is one way students can start to plan how their stories will unfold.

Students may also share photographs or illustrations with classmates and ask them what they see in the pictures in order to get an idea of what viewers still need to be told about in the text. This step may also come later in the process, as students develop and focus their draft.

At this point, writers often begin to work in circles through the writing process, rather than in straight lines. As students collect details and art, they may be prompted to go back and focus in a different way and may then collect more information or different art to go with the changed focus.

Research on the Web

Given that not all Web sites are appropriate for young people, some teachers I've worked with give students URLs for specific Web sites they want them to use, sites they've already checked out.

If you're having students look for Web sites on their own, talk with them about how they can tell if a Web site is a reliable source. There are a few things students can look for: Is there a link labeled "About" where you can get information about who put the information on the Web site? Is there a link to use to contact the person or persons who run the site? Is it easy to tell where the information on the site comes from? If not, the site might not be reliable; people providing good information should let you know who they are and where they got that information. Are there a lot of misspellings and other mistakes on the site? Those are also signs that the Web site might not be a great one to use for research. Talking about these issues can make students more savvy about what they see and read online. This kind of research also provides an opportunity to talk to students about copyright and fair use. (See "About Fair Use and Copyright" in Chapter 2.)

. . . .

Begin Writing

Now students start a draft, coming up with beginnings and thinking about where the stories will go from there. They can continue brainstorming, mapping, or freewriting. They can also keep gathering or creating art for their stories. If students are having trouble getting started with the writing, have them try one of these exercises:

- Get students to tell the stories aloud to other students. Talking it out may help them get ready for the writing. Often when we talk something out, we say things we didn't expect or are able to work through a problem.

- Have students quickly freewrite a draft in ten minutes. They'll have a draft done, taking away the fear that they have nothing to say, and they can revise as much as they want.

- Ask them to quickly write several titles that include different details or come at the stories from different angles or different points of view. What they come up with may help them see what they really want to focus on.

- Have students ask themselves questions about their audience and what writers do: What one thing does my audience need to know? What one thing does my audience need to know first? What surprised me about this subject? What would make my audience pay attention right away—a surprise, a problem to be solved, a description? They don't have to think about the audience if that's too overwhelming. Instead, they can imagine specific people they'd like to tell their stories to, friends or family members.

- If they're going to create illustrations for their stories, have them draw the first picture they think they'll use. This may get the writing going.

A Little Planning

At this point in the process, students may do a little planning before they go forward with the writing. If a student has a beginning point, he or she might brainstorm where to end the story, then list three or four points to include in the middle of the story: facts or actions or details that matter to the story. Don Murray calls these three or four points a trail (Murray 2002). This works as an outline to guide a student's writing, though the writer can change the story some as he or she continues through the process. Another quick outline students can create is a list of questions the story will answer. Once they've got the list, they can put the questions in an order that makes sense, considering what a reader has to know first, and next, and next. If a story is going to unfold in chronological order, writers can make a time line listing what happens first, and then what happens next. If writers have an ending but not a beginning, they can work backward, figuring out what to tell the viewers before the ending so the story will make sense.

Before students work on their own, you might have them create an outline using one of these formats—beginning/ending/three points (trail), questions, or time line—for a book they've read or a digital story they've watched, so they can talk about what the writer included and why, what came first, what came last, and what was most important and/or interesting. You might choose one of these outlines and have students create one as a class or in groups, working with a topic they know. Fiction or personal narrative may lend itself more to a time line, while nonfiction might lend itself more to a trail or questions. But these outlines can work with any genre.

As students are working through this process, writing beginnings and outlining, they're working on focus, the main messages they want to get across or the questions their stories will answer. It may be helpful if you can conference with students individually at this point, to see where they are headed. You might ask them to tell you, verbally or in writing, what their story is about, in one or two sentences only. If the sentences don't get to the heart of the story, you could ask questions to help the students figure out what should be in those sentences, so they tell something important about the story or from the story.

Organization

You might also want to discuss ways students can organize information in their stories: by taking viewers on a tour, by describing a process, by following chronology, or by relating a problem and then the solution. For example, if they look at Josh's story about his dog Logan (see "Josh Logan" on CD), they'll find Josh is loosely following a chronology, taking us through the dog's day. He begins with Logan introducing himself and his "people," but then we follow Logan on a walk (during which he gets petted, picks up a bottle, and barks at the post office), then home to his crate for a nap, then on another walk, then through dinnertime, on another walk in the rain, ending with what is supposed to be his bedtime.

Lizzie, though, has four pets she wants to introduce us to, so she takes us on a "tour" of the animals (see "Lizzie Moxie" on CD), featuring one photograph of each and one piece of narration for each. For her story about three wishes, first-grader Kristina follows a chronology but also includes a problem and solution (see "The Three Wishes" on CD).

Keep Writing

At this stage in the writing process, students develop a whole draft of their script. They may do this by freewriting or following a plan they made. They may conference with you or with peers on the developing scripts. The youngest children may first narrate their stories aloud to you. Remember that the stories don't have to be—shouldn't be—long, ranging from a paragraph to a page or page and a half, or several lines of a poem.

One way to help students keep the stories short, besides limiting the number of images you want them to use, is to have them think about what teachers in my classes have called "exploding the narrative." This basically means taking one part of a narrative and writing in detail about that small (but probably important) part, rather than telling the whole story from start to finish with the amount of detail the same for each part of the story. For example, when third-grader Luke writes about what happened when he went sledding, he starts by giving us a little context: "One cold afternoon it was a perfect day for sledding. So Dad took us to the sledding place." But after this he moves to the main thing he's writing about: the last sledding run of the day. "I wanted to go down one more time. So I did. At the top, I aimed for the bump at the bottom of the hill." Luke goes flying into the air after hitting the bump and collides with a snowboarder, and "it really hurt." He ends his story by saying, "I learned a good lesson: Beware of snowboarders."

To help students explode their narratives, you might ask them to choose the most important or interesting or dramatic part of their drafts, then write only about that for a few minutes. You might suggest they come up with sensory details or a really detailed description, or think about how they felt at the time they are writing about.

This writing may also move students beyond saying, "My story is about the red squirrel" or "My story is about my trip to California," and then reciting a list of facts about squirrels or "first we did this, then we did this, then..." Instead, they can be thinking and writing about the main message or messages they want to get across *about* the subject, what they most want their audience to know *about* the subject. You might talk with students and find out what one main thing they want other people to understand or take away from the stories, or what they think might be most interesting to classmates who don't know their stories yet or why they decided to write about this subject in the first place. This is where a student can think about that element of a digital story, the interesting question he or she wants the story to answer, and you might even ask what that question is.

Earlier I suggested having students tell, in one or two sentences, what the story is about. They might try that at this point in the process too. If a student writes, "My story is about my grandmother," you or other students can ask, "What do you want us to know about your grandmother?" or "What makes your grandmother special?" or "What did your grandmother do on the day you're writing about?" If the student writes, "My story is about red squirrels and their habitat," you or your students can ask, "What did you find really interesting about the red squirrel?" "Did anything you learn surprise you?" "What can you tell us about the red squirrel that we might not know?" "What is special about the red squirrel's habitat?"

More Questions to Help Build the Draft

You may also want to have students ask themselves one or more questions to develop their drafts, questions that also aim to get students to focus on their central messages or ideas: What happened and why? Why should people pay attention to this? What makes this interesting or funny or important? What do I know about this subject that most others wouldn't know? What made me laugh? What made me sad? What made me happy? What can I describe that will help tell the story? What do I remember best? What sounds, smells, tastes, touch, and sights do I remember? What are my pictures going to tell and what is my text going to tell?

Great Beginnings and Endings

What makes for a great beginning to a story? A strong beginning grabs readers' or viewers' attention somehow and makes them want to continue on. How? You can talk to students about different possibilities. You might tell students they don't have to start at the very beginning of the day or event they're writing about. ("I woke up and brushed my teeth, then got dressed.") Sometimes the action in the story is so compelling that all a student has to do is start the story at an interesting place, maybe just before something important happens. ("Carrying my fishing gear, I stepped onto the ice and headed toward the middle of the pond. Then I heard a cracking sound.") Students can always backtrack with a phrase like "that morning" or "earlier that day" if there's something earlier in time viewers need to know about.

Sometimes a surprising fact can draw readers in; so can an intriguing quote from a character in the story, or a description of the place where the action happens or that includes vivid sensory details the writer remembers. You might have students write a few different beginnings using some of these elements to see what might work best.

"Bunny Tales" by third-grader Emma (see "Bunny Tales" on CD) starts with an intriguing statement that makes us want to know more: "I'm Charlie and I'm Snowball, and we want to tell you how we got adopted in a weird sort of way." Fourth-grader Kyler's story about a particular animal begins with a question to grab the audience: "Have you ever seen a pointy-nosed mouse? It's a common tree shrew." Kristina's three wishes story (see "The Three Wishes" on CD) starts right in with the important information: "Kristina and Krissy were sitting in Jamaica, wishing that they could be rich and have lots of dogs." All three authors present the main subject of the story right away.

And what makes a great ending to a story? The endings students write should clearly finish the stories so that we don't expect them to go on, and the same things that make good beginnings can make good endings. I tell my journalism students they don't want to just sum up what they've already said in the story at the end. Instead, they want to leave their readers with one more new piece of information, and maybe remind us of where the story started. Students can ask themselves these questions: What picture—literally and in words—do I want to leave the audience with? What do I want the audience to know at the end? What's the last thing the audience needs to know? What's the last thing I want to say?

As with beginnings, you might have students write several endings and choose ones that best bring their stories full circle and say what they want to say. If they already wrote several beginnings, you might have them try them out as endings, to see if any of them would work.

Third-grader Ana's fairy tale about three elephants and a wizard finishes with a simple ending that ties things up. The three elephants start the story wishing they had wings so they could fly to Greece. They ask a wizard for help, but the wizard is evil and gives them wings that don't work. The elephants steal the wand and fix their wings. The story ends, "They returned the wand and had a wonderful time at the beach," the beach being, of course, in Greece. Josh's story about his dog Logan (see "Josh Logan" on CD) ends with the dog, who is shut in the kitchen by a gate, knocking the gate down and saying, "I am the champion! Booyah!" This is a great ending because it fits the rambunctious critter we've been introduced to in the story.

Be Specific

Since these stories are so short, concrete language and details that surprise can really make a story fly. For example, in Josh's story (see "Josh Logan" on CD), we find out his dog Logan thinks his food is made of "sweet molecules and peppermint"—I love knowing that. Meredith wrote a story about a saucer race between Moon aliens and Mars aliens. She tells us the Mars aliens "were green. Their arms were made of wax and their legs were made of staples," while Moon aliens "were 18 feet tall and weighed 400 pounds. They had legs of slime and arms of spaghetti. They had toes but not fingers." In Lizzie's story about her pets (see "Lizzie Moxie" on CD), we find out that one of her cats, Duke, is scared of "the ding-dong sound." The authors use vivid details to make us see and hear. You might ask students to consider what makes the main subject of their story different from other pets or places or people or whatever, to ask themselves questions about sensory details, or to think again about what surprises them about their subjects. They might think about details that really stick with them from their favorite books as examples of the kinds of details they might include in their own stories.

Word Play, Similes, and Metaphors

I'm a poet, and I love the richness of our language. Encourage your students to play with language when they're doing any kind of writing. I have my favorite words: *luminous, silvery,* and *azure.* Have students make lists of their favorite words, just to get them thinking beyond the usual. I tell my students to think particularly about words that sound like what they mean: *pop, giggle, strut, grumble, whack,* and *gush.* I'm not saying students should strain to use unusual words in their stories, but you can suggest ways to go beyond the language they might usually use. You can even pull out a thesaurus and read them synonyms for, say, the verb *walk: pace, march, plod, stalk, shuffle,* or *lope.*

For example, in first-grader Matthew's story about Humboldt penguins (see "Penguins in Action" on CD), the mother penguin doesn't just jump out of the water, she "porpoises out." She doesn't walk, she "waddles." In Josh's story (see "Josh Logan" on CD), Logan the dog doesn't just get tired, he gets "tuckered out."

Similes and metaphors can add surprises and meaning to a digital story. With these, writers compare and contrast two different things; their meanings collide and create something new. You might get groups of students, or the whole class, to think of sayings like "soft as a feather" or "hard as a rock" or "busy as a bee" and then create new ones: It was as hard as the water feels when you do a belly flop into the pool. They were as busy as a bunch of hockey players fighting for a puck.

If students are starting with abstract words, like *happiness* or *peace*, they might create metaphors by comparing those abstract words to concrete things, or vice versa. In one of my poems I have this phrase, "my love an egg in your keeping." I was thinking about how fragile love can be.

Show and Tell

We often tell writers to show rather than tell, and it's good advice, though stories usually need some of both. What we mean when we ask writers to show is that rather than simply saying something like, "My dog was really happy" or "It was a spooky night," writers should paint a picture readers can see in their heads by providing the evidence, action, or details that make readers know the dog was happy or think the night was spooky: "My dog jumped up and down and licked our faces." "The clouds streamed across the orange moon, and the wind howled like a lonely coyote." In Sarah's digital story about apples being made into applesauce (see "Sarah and Apple" on CD), for example, she doesn't say the apple is scared of getting cooked. She has the apple cry out, "Oh, stop, please, no, not me, save me, help!"

To have students practice showing, not telling, you might give them some basic sentences, such as "Tim got angry when his sister teased him" or "Mary had a crazy day at school." Then you can ask them to write sentences that show how you'd know Tim was angry (he stomped his feet and slammed his bedroom door) or Mary had a crazy day (she accidentally let the class guinea pigs loose, then somebody spilled paint on her, and when she opened her lunchbox she found that her mother switched her lunch with her father's, so she had liverwurst). You can have them do this as a whole class, in groups or pairs, or on their own. After they've finished, have them look through their drafts to see if there's any place they might be able to show instead of tell.

With digital stories, as I mentioned in Chapter 2, the images as well as the words "show," so writers will want to keep that in mind, making the text and images work together, each one adding to and clarifying the story line. Many of the images students use will probably illustrate the text, as when, in his gentle dog and fierce hamster story (see "Nathan Hamster" on CD), second-grader Nathan has the dog give the hamster a fish, and the picture that goes with the narration shows exactly that. But images can help set the mood of the story—if the colors are bright, the mood of the story may be cheerful, while if the pictures are dark or of something menacing (like a tornado) the mood will likely be somber. And the pictures may demonstrate something the text does not explain. In her Bunny Tales story (see "Bunny Tales" on CD), Emma tells us that two bunnies pictured eating flowers in a meadow "wanted to try to go where the people live, to try to find an owner. So we did, but it didn't work out well because . . ." The next picture comes up and the narration continues, "We got caught. We didn't know that being adopted would be this scary." The picture shows what this means—it's a pet carrier, all closed up, and "Ahhhhhhhh" in a dialogue balloon coming out of the carrier.

Transitions in Writing

Some students might work on transitions and connectors when writing their scripts. How will students move through their stories? Will they use transitional words and phrases such as "next" or "later that day" or even "moving along . . ."? Will they connect the different parts through repetition of a word or phrase or a synonym of a word already used—a connector? For example, a student might start one section with, "This is my dog, Willow." The next section might start "My dog" or "Willow" or "My pet," connecting the two sections.

When students put the stories together in the computer, they'll also have a chance to create visual transitions between the individual images that help make up that story. One student whose story featured family and pets made transitions/connections with words and images: The first picture and first part of her story were about her dad, who she tells us was the one who usually feeds the dog; the dog is then featured in the second picture and second part of the story, and she tells us the dog plays with the cat; the cat is featured in the third picture and section of the story, and so on.

Looking at transitions and connectors in books they've read is one way to get students to think about how to move from one part of a story to another.

Once students have finished their drafts, they may need to go back and collect or create more images or different images to go with the story. When they've got all their images together (though they can add or delete images right up to the last step of finishing the story) and a script pretty much set, they can move on to the next part of drafting a digital story—figuring out how the words and images will come together.

Storyboarding

The process of writing a digital story requires a task that other writing doesn't—storyboarding. Storyboarding is figuring out what section of text goes with what piece of art, and so it also entails splitting the story or script up into parts. It's another way of thinking through the stories. Students can do this in a number of ways. A storyboard can be as simple as a piece of paper listing each image in the story and then what text goes with each image. There are also templates you can download from the Web for students to use. Look at digital storytelling Web sites to find templates—for example, the Educational Uses of Digital Storytelling, Digitales, or Integrating Digital Storytelling in Your Classroom (see the Web sites listed in the "References and Resources" section at the end of the book). Many templates are 8-by-12-inch rectangles covered with big squares in rows with lines beneath each square. Students write in the squares which photograph or picture goes first, then next, and so on. Underneath the squares, they write the text that goes with each piece of art, and maybe even what music they are going to use, if they know at this point.

In two third-grade classes I worked with, the teachers gave the students 8-by-10-inch paper copies of their images, and the students did storyboarding by writing the appropriate text on the back of each copy.

A great way to storyboard is to use sticky notes. Give students sticky notes and a big piece of paper and have them write the subjects of their art on individual sticky notes, one for each piece of art. Once they've split their story into sections, have them write the sections of text onto the paper and then, using the sticky notes, match each piece of art with each section of text. The sticky notes make it easy to move the art around or add new art—which may take students back to the research part of the process. The students may also find they need or want to change their script to work better with their art or to tell a part of the story they hadn't thought of before. Some students get into this part of the process because it seems more active to them than simply sitting and writing or trying to revise by just going through their text again.

One teacher I worked with had students use sticky notes in another way. She had them write out their whole script, then write each piece of it on a sticky note along with a notation about which piece of art went with each piece of text. This helped them decide if they had the right art and also whether they wanted to use all of their text, and it also gave them ideas about what else they might want to say in their scripts or what other visual images they needed to collect to make their stories complete. Again, the writing process folds in on itself here, with students going back to collecting or even to focusing.

Photo Story 3 doesn't allow you to record one continuous voice track. For each piece of art, you must record just that piece of story individually. So before recording their narration, students must have some version of the written script clearly split into parts, so that they know when each piece of story begins and ends. Students can draw lines between the different parts right on their drafts or write the different parts on sticky notes, on the back of the pictures they've made or printouts of photographs they are using, or on individual sheets of paper, one for each piece of story. It's best if students don't have to turn pages during the recording, since the microphone will pick up that sound.

More Questions, More Showing and Telling

More questions can help students figure out how to storyboard as well as whether they need to do any revising: Which image goes best with which part of the story, and why? What does this part of my story say, and do I need and have an image to help explain this part? What should my first image be if I want to grab my viewers? Does it work with the beginning of my story? Do some of the images show things the text doesn't tell but that are still important to the story? Do I need more images or different images? Do I need to rewrite part of the story so it goes better with the image?

It's fine if students revise their stories right up until they finish putting everything together on the computer. While they are storyboarding, and even while they are putting the art and text together on the computer, students may continue to make changes. Students will often rewrite their scripts to fit the images better, decide they need other images to go with their script, or move images and parts of their stories around. I've been amazed at how much rewriting and reworking goes on, at this stage and at the next. One third-grade teacher I worked with, Debbie Finch, of Windham, New Hampshire, said, "They don't see all the rewriting they've done. They say to me at the end, 'This is so easy.' They don't realize what went into the final product because the final product is so satisfying to them" (2009a).

One youngster I helped had written a story about the members of her family, telling facts about them, their likes and dislikes, but when she came in to record her narration, she told me she didn't have an ending yet and didn't know how to finish her story. I suggested she think about what she wanted us to know by the end; she said she wanted us to know how she felt about her family. Then she wrote a paragraph describing that, to complete the story, and we did the recording. Another youngster was creating a story about making a Webcast with her friend. She came in to record but wasn't happy with the photographs she had for one point of the story where she and her friends were dancing. We looked through clip art until we found a dancing image that she thought would work, one that included the right number of people in it.

The students know these stories will be shown to others, and they want to make their stories clear and interesting and *satisfying*, for them and for viewers. That means the images and words must work well together to say just what each writer wants to say. These writers want their individual voices to be heard through the words they choose, and to tell stories no one else can tell.

Taking Students Through the Writing Process: Part Two

*I have heard the power of kids' voices and realize that [digital storytelling]
is just the next step in what we are already doing. In my primary classroom we
often work with art (drawing, papier-mâché models, collage, paintings, photographs
of us in field trip settings) first. These images or models fit beautifully into the
storyboard model that we already use as a map. We will just take it one step
further by preserving the child's voice in that moment in time that makes the
written word and image even more compelling.*

—Mary Jo Gregg, second-grade teacher, Exeter, New Hampshire

There is one scene in the movie *E. T.* that always makes me smile. The little guy from outer space is holed up inside a kid's bedroom because the kid's mom isn't supposed to know E.T. is in the house. One morning she hears a noise upstairs and goes to investigate. She opens the closet door where—gasp!—we viewers know E.T. is probably hiding. The camera pans across the closet right to left, across a huge pile of stuffed animals and dolls—with E.T.'s face right in the middle of them. The mother doesn't notice him amid all those toy faces and closes the door. It's a small moment but really funny.

The movies students make when they're creating digital stories don't come near the complexity of *E. T.*—though they may make you laugh too—but the basic moviemaking principles are the same, and you may want to explore a favorite movie with your students before they go further in the process to see what techniques they think help tell a story and how. Zooming in and zooming out, for instance, are ways a movie director focuses our attention on something or surprises us with the big picture. Panning, having the camera move across a scene, gives a sense of movement and maybe of space and can surprise us, as that moment in *E. T.* does. Your young directors already know some of this stuff intuitively. Get them to use what they know when making their digital stories.

. . . .

Finish Writing

The last step of the writing process—finish writing—includes the moviemaking: getting the images into the software program, putting them in order, adding titles, adding special effects to the pictures and transitions between the pictures, recording the narration, adding music, and revising until the stories are just as the students want them to be. I'll show you now how to take students through this last step using Microsoft Photo Story 3 for Windows. (Even if students are using a more complicated program such as Movie Maker or iMovie, which work differently than Photo Story 3, they'll go through the same set of tasks to create digital stories, and it's not too hard to figure out how to accomplish those tasks. Movie Maker, for example, offers on-screen help all the way through. There are also many tutorials online to help you with these programs. Do a Google search for "tutorial" and the name of the software to find them. One Web site that lists links to iMovie tutorials is http://co-bw.com/Tutorial%20IMovie%20Links.htm; check out http://its.leesummit.k12.mo.us/digitalmedia.htm for links to some Movie Maker tutorials.)

Photo Story 3 is simple and easy to learn. It also features on-screen help all the way through the process. While I can't promise you'll never run into a computer glitch, you'll find Photo Story 3 as foolproof as it gets. If you end up using a different program and do run into a problem, there's lots of help available online. Check out the Web site of Classroom 2.0 (http://www.classroom20.com), a social network for teachers interested in using technology in the classroom, or the EDTECH electronic mailing list (http://www.h-net.org/~edweb), an online discussion group that discusses educational technology issues. Look at the digital storytelling Web sites I've suggested in Chapter 2, and look at the sites they link to. Demonstrate the software to your students one step at a time.

Get Help

This part of the process can be pretty disorderly, because not everyone will work through every step in the same amount of time, and there will probably come a moment when every student will want your help at exactly the same time. No matter what grade you're working with, get as much help as you can on computer days from aides or parents or older students. First and second graders especially may need one-on-one help to work with Photo Story 3. I have assisted as many as fifteen third-grade students at a time by myself (and was a little loopy by the end of it, but they got their stories done); older students, once they've seen the program demonstrated, should be able to work through it pretty easily on their own.

Just as students can mentor one another through the writing, they can help one another with the computers. One afternoon I worked with third graders in a lab, walking around behind them as they put together their digital stories, answering questions here and there. I saw one student gazing at her neighbor's computer screen; the young man beside her was adding transitions to his story. "How do you do that?" she asked. "I can show you," he said. He showed her, and she showed someone else, and pretty soon most of the students were experimenting with transitions. They didn't need me anymore.

You may want to create a chart for the whole class or individual worksheets outlining the different steps students will go through, so you and they can track where they are in the process. You could list the steps as follows: writing script; drawing pictures (or taking photographs or finding art online); matching parts of the story with pieces of art; importing and arranging art; making a title slide; recording narration; and creating music.

How Much Computer Work Should Students Do?

The more students do to prepare their images and text for the digital stories and then put them together on the computer, the more invested they will be in the stories. Let them do as much as they can, from typing their scripts into the computer to figuring out the order their pictures and text will go in to choosing transitions between the art to creating their own music.

With younger students, as I mentioned in Chapter 3, you may decide to do all of the computer work yourself or perhaps even to create a group project rather than individual stories. Whatever will work best for you and your students will be fine. Even if you do much of the computer work the first time around, students will have that satisfaction of hearing their own voices reading their words.

I want to show you all the possibilities this program offers. But if the detailed instructions I give you in this chapter seem to be more involved than your students are ready for or just more involved than you want them to get, you can simplify this part of the process too. Students need only go through three steps with the program to create their stories: importing images; arranging images in the right order; and recording the narration that goes with each image.

How Many Computers?

This part of the process goes most smoothly if you have access to a computer lab, stationary or portable. Then all students in a class can be working on the computers at the same time. But if that's not your situation, you can still do these stories and make the project manageable.

Suppose you have access to only a couple of computers. Perhaps you can designate one as the computer students can use to import and work with their images (and perhaps to add transitions between those images and to create music to go with their stories) and the other as the one students will use to record the narration. (Hopefully that second computer is in a quiet spot.) Even if you have enough computers for every student, you might want to pair students up when they start their computer work so they can help each other through it and cheer each other on.

Because Photo Story 3 is simple to use, students and teachers I've worked with have rarely run into problems with it in a lab. One problem we've encountered, however, is students who don't save their stories in the right place and "lose" them as a result. School computer systems are not all the same, so the way to solve this problem is going to vary from one school to another. If you're going to have students save their work-in-progress on your school system computers, you might make sure each student has a file, labeled with his or her name, into which the student saves downloaded photos, other artwork, the script, music if it's downloaded, and the actual Photo Story project. Otherwise, chaos! Another way to keep students from misplacing their Photo Story projects is to have them use their name as part of the project name, like "Sam Lucy" or "Jungle Mikayla," and write down the name they choose. That way if they don't save the project in the right place, you may be able to search for it on the computer system.

I've run into two other problems. Occasionally, I've had trouble getting a certain microphone to work with a certain computer, for no reason I could figure out. Swapping microphones usually solves the problem. If students are recording on a laptop, the built-in microphone will work fine. The other problem I've run into has to do with how long each image is displayed, and I'll discuss this later in this chapter (see page 69).

Start with the Images

Before students can create their stories in Photo Story 3, their artwork must be converted to digital form—picture files with the suffix *jpg* or *gif.* I suggest using the jpg format for photographs, and the gif format for simpler images that are made up of type or solid colors. (Photo Story actually accepts many types of image files, but these two are probably the most common.) If your students have used digital cameras, you can download their photographs right into the computer; if they've used disposable digital cameras, you can have CDs made up of the photos rather than prints. Either way, the pictures will be in the right format. You can use a scanner to scan them into the computer too, and this is one way to get students' original artwork in the computer. Whether you do the downloading or scanning or have students do it will depend on the availability of the scanner and the skills of the students. It can take a lot of time if you yourself have to scan in four or five pictures for each student. Instead you can take digital photographs of the students' artwork and then download those photos. This takes less time than scanning, and the quality of the photographs is fine for use with Photo Story 3.

Altering the Photographs

If you want, you can have older students alter their photographs—cropping them, for example—in a program such as Adobe Photoshop. This will add more time to the process and isn't required. But if you need to teach such skills to your students, this is the time in the process to do it. Photo Story 3 allows minimal cropping and addition of special effects to pictures, but a program such as Photoshop will do much more. I'd stay away from too much photo altering unless, as I said, you want students to learn how to use a program that goes into more detail than Photo Story 3.

If a student is going to crop a photo, he or she should do it to make the focus of the photograph clearer, to make something in the photo stand out more, or to get rid of extraneous information, being careful not to crop off people's heads or arms or legs, which just looks strange.

● ●

Photo Story 3: The First Steps

Before your students work with the program themselves, you'll probably want to demonstrate it to the whole group. If you can hook up one computer to a projector or TV, have students gather round and watch as you go through each step. If you must do the demonstration in the lab, while students are sitting in front of computer terminals, don't let them boot up the computers until after you've given your demonstration.

Once you're ready to have them use the program, it's helpful to list on a board the steps you want them to take, in the order you want them to follow. For example, your list might say "import art, add transitions, create music." You may want to have all students complete one step before anyone moves on to another, though it can be hard to keep students from moving ahead! As I mentioned previously, if students are working at their own pace, a way to keep track of each student's progress is to create a chart—either a class chart or individual ones for each student—with students' names and the tasks you want them to accomplish; then have them check off each step as they complete it.

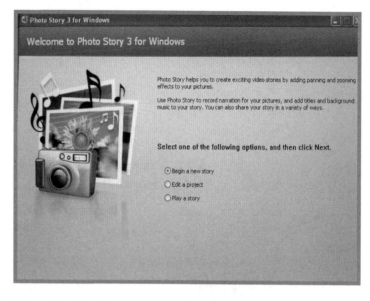

Figure 4.1 Photo Story 3 opening screen

Microsoft Digital Story 3 screen shots reprinted with permission from Microsoft Corporation.

Your students will have these elements to work with: their artwork, which is already in the computer, and their script. They should begin by double-clicking on the Photo Story 3 program icon to start up the program. They will get an opening screen (see Figure 4.1) that allows them to select one of the following: begin a new story, edit a project (one that's already begun), or play a story.

When they choose Begin a New Story, and click on the button Next, they will get another screen, the Import and Arrange Your Pictures screen (see Figure 4.2), which will allow them to begin by importing the artwork they're going to use. All of the main screens from this one to the last one will now feature a Help button, a Save Project button, and Back, Next, and Cancel buttons. Students will use the Next button to move to the next screen and tasks and the Back button to go back a screen. The Cancel button can be used to shut down the program; if they click on that button, students will be prompted to save any changes they've made to their stories before the program closes.

Students now click on the button labeled Import Pictures, and they'll be prompted to browse the computer to find the folder with their art in it. Then they can import all the art. They can click on and highlight one piece of art, click OK, and the art should show up along the bottom of the Photo Story 3 screen on what is called the film strip. (See Figure 4.2. The numbers on top of the pictures in the film strip are the number of seconds the narration lasts for each picture.) Sarah had already recorded her narration when this photo was taken. Your students won't see such numbers until they record.) They can import more than one piece of art at a time by highlighting several of them at once—by holding down the shift key and clicking on each piece until all the pieces wanted are highlighted.

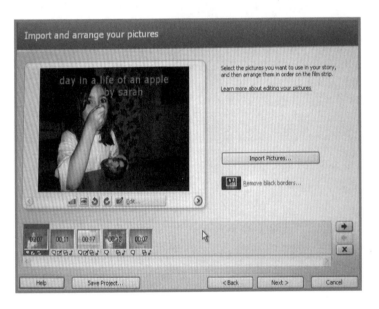

Figure 4.2 Import and Arrange Your Pictures screen
Microsoft Digital Story 3 screen shots reprinted with permission from Microsoft Corporation.

Once their art is imported, students can then change the order of the art by clicking on and dragging one piece or another to the right place on the film strip. If they want to delete a picture they've imported, they can right click on it and choose the Delete option. They can import and/or delete pictures the entire time they are working on the project—one way they'll revise as they go along.

They'll also have the option to use the Remove Black Borders button, which will allow them to do just that. The program will put black borders around photos that don't match a ratio of width to height of 4:3. You can have students ignore this and continue with the black borders, remove the borders now, or remove the black borders at some other point in the project.

Have students save the project after they've imported their photos; have them save it every time they make changes to their story. What they're doing is saving it as a Photo Story 3 project file with a *wp3* suffix, meaning they can open the project up again and change it. Make sure they've saved the project in the same place they've saved their art so everything is together, in case they need to re-import a piece of art or add a new piece.

Figure 4.3 Main Crop screen

Microsoft Digital Story 3 screen shots reprinted with permission from Microsoft Corporation.

Optional Editing

The Import and Arrange Your Pictures screen allows students to do several things, all optional. To keep things simple, you may not want your students to mess with this stuff; just have them click the Next button to move along. If you want them to try it out, students must first click on one of the photos in the film strip; the one they click on becomes the featured photo they'll work with, and it shows up in the upper left box. Then they can click on any of the four boxes or the Edit button that appear below that photograph. The first box adjusts the color, the second corrects red-eye, and the other two allow you to rotate the photographs one way or the other.

If students click on the Edit button, they'll have the option of cropping the photograph (see Figure 4.3). If they then click on the little box labeled Crop, they'll be able to cut out part of the featured photograph, or change the focus of it by

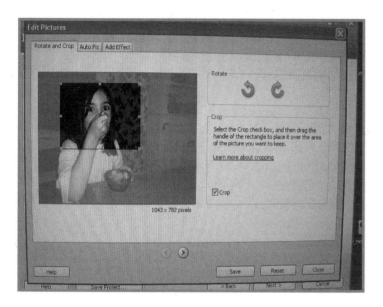

Figure 4.4 Detailed Crop screen

Microsoft Digital Story 3 screen shots reprinted with permission from Microsoft Corporation.

zooming in on only one part (see Figure 4.4).

If students click on the Auto Fix tab at the top left of the main crop screen, they have another chance to correct color levels and red-eye as well as contrast. If they click on Add Effect, they can change the appearance of the photograph in several ways. But they'll get another chance to do this on the Add a Title to Your Pictures screen coming up next, so I'd just have students move on from here.

When they close down the Crop screens and click on the Next button, if they haven't removed black borders from their images, they will get a dialogue box that asks whether they want to continue with the pictures as they are or remove the borders. Unless you want students to spend some time with this, tell them to click on the Yes button and keep going. As I said earlier, they can go back later in the process and remove the black borders if they wish.

Add Titles and Effects to Pictures

This next screen, the Add a Title to Your Pictures screen, allows students to do two things: type text that will appear on pictures and add special effects to the pictures (see Figure 4.5). Again, they must click on the pictures they want to work with, one at a time. There's a little box next to the featured picture with a message that says "Type text to add a title on the selected picture." Whatever students type in will appear on the slide. This is how they can make title and credit slides; some students will also want to put text on other pieces of artwork in their story. For example, third-grader Grace put a caption, "Zzzzz," on the picture of her dog snoozing to emphasize what's going on at that point in her digital story (see "Grace Willow" on CD). On pictures of her cats and dog, classmate Lizzie put the name of each pet on that animal's picture so the audience would be absolutely certain who they were hearing about at any point in the story (see "Lizzie Moxie" on CD).

Students should think about whether text on the pictures will help viewers understand the pictures or add to the text in some way. If not, they don't need to put text on any slides except the first one, for the title, and maybe one at the end for credits. (See Resource Box: Text-Only Slides for information on how to create text-only slides.)

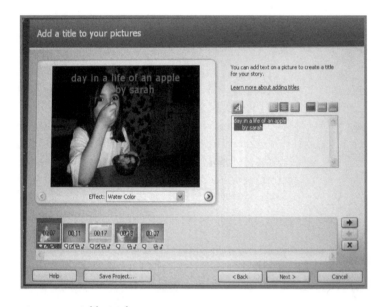

Figure 4.5 Add a Title to Your Pictures screen
Microsoft Digital Story 3 screen shots reprinted with permission from Microsoft Corporation.

RESOURCE BOX: TEXT-ONLY SLIDES

Photo Story 3 does not allow students to create images; it allows them only to import already existing images. If students want to include slides that have text on them but no image, students will have to use another program to do it. Students can create text-only slides in Microsoft PowerPoint and then save them, not as slides but as jpg or gif files, using the pulldown menu that comes up when they choose the Save As option. Then they can import these jpg or gif files just as they did their other pictures.

On the Add a Title to Your Picture screen, the little button with the two letter As on it will let students change the font, font size, font color, and type of script for the text. (See Figure 4.6 to see what comes up when you click on this font button.) The three little buttons next to it allow students to left-justify, center, or right-justify the text on the photo. The last three buttons allow them to change the position of the text: top, middle, or bottom.

The Effect menu, right under the featured picture, includes ten ways students can alter the appearance of their artwork: black and white; chalk and charcoal; colored pencil; diffuse glow; negative; outline, black; outline, grey; sepia; washout; and water color (see Figure 4.7).

Students will have fun with these and will spend some time trying them out. OK, they may waste some time playing with these. You can turn an ordinary photograph or drawing into an abstract painting. Some children will choose a certain effect just because they like the look; a few students have told me they chose different effects for each photograph in their stories because they thought that would make their audience really pay attention. It is a great way to keep all photographs from looking the same. But you can tell your students that less is more here; they don't want the pictures to look so strange that it's hard to figure out what they are, drawing too much attention away from the story they have to tell.

They have the option of adding titles or effects to each individual picture, one at a time. They can move quickly from one picture to another by using the arrows that appear below the featured picture in the screen.

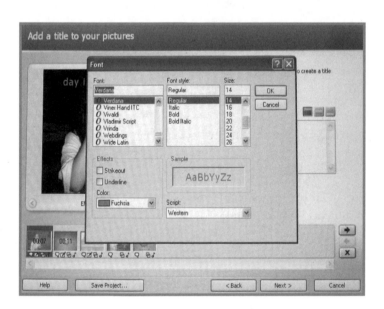

Figure 4.6 Font choices

Microsoft Digital Story 3 screen shots reprinted with permission from Microsoft Corporation.

Next Up: Movement and Transitions

Photo Story 3 also allows students to control movement across a picture, so they can zoom in or out or pan across or up and down. It also allows them to introduce different transitions—visual changes such as having one picture fade out and the next one fade in—between pictures.

Students can skip this part of the process; they don't have to use the movement or transition features. In Photo Story 3 there are default settings; if you or your students do not choose certain movement or transitions, the program chooses for you. It may be best with the youngest

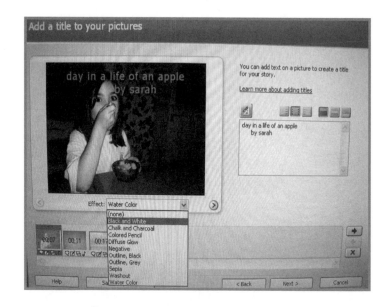

Figure 4.7 Effect menu

Microsoft Digital Story 3 screen shots reprinted with permission from Microsoft Corporation.

students to go with the default selections. But older students will have a great time turning their text and art into movies by experimenting with these options. They'll also use both their words and pictures as transitions through their digital stories.

Many students already have a good sense of basic moviemaking (or TV-show-making) techniques. They know a moviemaker zooms in tight on an object or person's face to emphasize it and make sure we see whatever's most important about the scene. They've seen different types of transitions between scenes, such as the fading out of one scene and the fading into another, so they know that there must be some connection between different elements in a story and a clear path from one to another, with their words and their visuals. All of this may give students ideas about the kinds of stories they want to tell and the ways they might tell them.

The movement across or up and down a picture can help signal what we should pay attention to. Have students think of this as a visual way, rather than a verbal way,

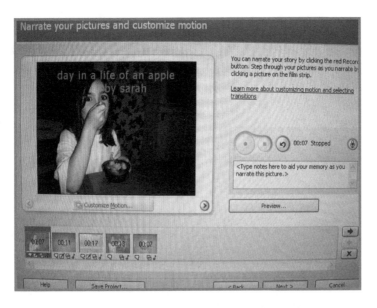

Figure 4.8 Narrate Your Pictures and Customize Motion screen
Microsoft Digital Story 3 screen shots reprinted with permission from Microsoft Corporation.

to tell us something is important or to make us pay attention.

For example, a third grader who wrote about a day in the life of her dog, as told by her dog, included one picture of him running out in the yard, with the narrator exclaiming how wonderful it was to feel the wind in his fur. The student panned across the picture to give the illusion of motion, to match what was going on in her story.

In Sam's story about his hamster, Lucy (see "Sam Lucy" on CD), all the photographs start as wide shots and then focus in on the hamster, except for one. That one starts with a close-up

of Lucy, then moves out, because we're not meant to know right away where Lucy is. The narrator says, "Man, this thing that I'm standing on is really stiff. I think there are two of them . . . Hey, there's my shadow. I think I am pretty high up." As the picture opens up, we see Lucy is sitting on a brick in the sun.

Zooming and Panning

To add transitions and movement to their stories, students should move from the Add a Title to Your Pictures screen (shown in Figure 4.5), clicking the Next button to get to the Narrate Your Pictures and Customize Motion screen (see Figure 4.8).

To zoom or pan, they should first click on the Customize Motion button and then on the Motion and Duration tab. To get out of the default settings the program automatically goes to, they must click the box labeled "Specify start and end position of motion." Tiny squares will appear on the sides and corners of the picture. Using these squares or handles, students can drag the sides or corners of the picture in or out or drag the square delineating the featured part of the photo to one part of the photo or another so that the view of the picture the audience will see moves from right to left or in or out (see Figure 4.9). For example, with the first picture of Sarah's apple story, if I wanted viewers to first see the whole picture and then focus on her face, I'd click on the "Specify start and end position of motion" box. Then I'd use the handles on the second photo on the screen, moving them and dragging the rectangle they create until the featured area of the photo is Sarah's face. I'd leave the first photo full screen. The photo will open showing the whole shot, then zoom in on her face.

From now on, during the customizing pictures and adding music stages, the Photo Story 3 screens feature a Preview button. If students click on the Preview button, they can see what they've chosen will look like and can change it if they wish. One of the things that makes this program easy to use is that they can always hit the Reset button if they want to start over.

Students have the option of setting the duration of the movement automatically or setting the number of seconds to display the picture. *It's important that students leave this one on automatic.* Remember earlier I

Figure 4.9 Motion and Duration screen
Microsoft Digital Story 3 screen shots reprinted with permission from Microsoft Corporation.

mentioned I'd run into problems with this? Photo Story 3 automatically displays each picture for as long as the recorded audio for each lasts. If students change the duration of the display of a picture, making display time different than the audio time, the program doesn't know how to handle this, and the story may not run properly. Automatic is the way to go, at least until after the audio is recorded. Some students will worry that some pictures don't stay up as long as they would like or stay up too long. Tell them they can adjust that after they record their audio.

As with titles and effects, they'll go through this process for each individual picture. Again, they can move quickly from one picture to another by using the arrows that appear below the featured picture in the screen.

Transitions

All transitions, verbal and visual, show some sort of relationship between one part of the story and another, whether it's a move from one step in a process or one fact to another, or a major switch in topic or circumstance.

When talking to students about visual transitions, you might remind them again that they don't want anything that's so distracting it gets in the way of telling their stories. Students enjoy experimenting with different transitions, and the program offers forty-eight of them. Younger students may just enjoy trying them all. You might talk with older students about the effects of the transitions they choose. Are they so flashy they take the attention away from the story?

The "crossfade" option (one picture fades into another) and the "fade to/from black" option (one picture fades to black, then that fades into the second picture) seem to me to create bigger breaks than some of the other transitions. It makes sense to use such transitions for a move to another time or place or subject. The student's narrative may indicate the same with phrases such as "later that day," or "meanwhile," or even "moving on."

Other transitions seem to indicate a more minor switch, maybe a move simply to the next step or action in the story. For example, with the "circle outward" transition, a circle appears in the center of the first picture, revealing a little of the second, and the circle then grows larger until the first picture is entirely eclipsed by the second. You can see parts of both transitions all the way through the transformation, so you see a relationship between the pictures. A verbal transition might simply be the words *next* or *after that*.

To insert transitions, students must first close the Customize Motion screen to get back to the Narrate and Customize Motion screen (Figure 4.8). They should then highlight the picture in the film strip that they want to transition to—for example, if students want to create a transition between the first and second picture on the film strip, they should click on the second picture. Then they can click on the Customize Motion button, and then the Transition tab again, to get to the Transition screen (see Figure 4.10).

They'll see three little boxes at the top of this screen, labeled "Previous picture," "Transition," and "Current picture." Because Sarah wanted to add a transition between the first and second pictures in her story, she highlighted the second picture

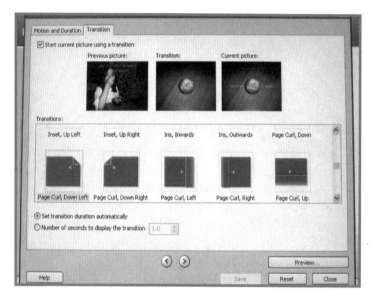

Figure 4.10 Transition screen

Microsoft Digital Story 3 screen shots reprinted with permission from Microsoft Corporation.

(the apple) on the film strip before moving to the Transition screen. In Figure 4.10, the apple picture shows up in the "Current picture" box, and the first picture on her film strip shows up in the "Previous picture" box. The transition will go in the middle.

The transition options are displayed under those three boxes on the Transition screen, and students can scroll through them to find the ones they want. Students click on their chosen transitions, and they'll see those they chose in motion in the "Transition" box. They can use the same transition between all pictures or choose different transitions for each pair of pictures. When a student finishes with one transition, he or she can click the Close button to get back to the Narrate the Pictures and Customize Motion screen again, highlight the next picture on the film strip, then click the Customize Motion button again to return to the Transition screen.

One second grader I met did a great job with one important transition. He wrote a story about two baseball players and a fairy who grants them three wishes. In the story, one ballplayer wishes he could bat really well. After he makes his wish, a live, flying black bat appears, not what he'd had in mind at all. His colleague wishes for a baseball bat to chase the live bat away, and then they wish for a baseball so they can play. A picture of the two players, with one holding the baseball bat, comes before a picture of the two players with the baseball flying through the air between them. The student used a "star, outwards" transition; when the illustration including the baseball first shows up on the screen, all we can see is a star-shaped part of the picture, the part showing the baseball. Then the star expands until we can see the whole picture. That student put the initial focus right on the baseball.

In third-grader Grace's story about her dog Willow (see "Grace Willow" on CD), the first slide features both Grace and Willow, and the narration (Willow is narrating) tells about what Grace likes to do with her dog. Then Grace uses a "flip" transition—it looks like the whole slide is flipping around—to make a fairly big change in subject, and her narration reflects that change: "Hi, I will tell you a little about me now."

Down at the bottom of the Transition screen students have the option of setting the number of seconds a transition lasts, rather than letting the program set this automatically. As with the duration of display of a picture, tell them to leave this on automatic, at least until they've completed more of the story. Students should wait until they record their audio and see how the story works before they make any changes in timing. Changing the timing of transitions is optional, of course. They can stay with the default setting.

Remember that all of this computer work is part of the Finish Writing part of the process, and the written text is still in play as students choose movement and transitions. They will revise their text to match the pictures; they may add or delete pictures, change transitions, or add or subtract text to make their story work better.

Recording the Voice-over

When students are done with all of the pictures, they're ready to record. Students will stay with the Narrate Your Pictures and Customize Motion screen to record narration. At this point, it's good if students have earphones so everyone doesn't have to listen to everyone else's voice-over and music (next step) while they are finishing up their stories. (If you want, you can have students go to the next screen, the Add

Background Music screen, add music, then come back to the recording later. If you have a limited number of computers or, say, just one set up to record, you could have individual students record while others work on their music—with earphones.)

To the right of the featured picture, students will see four buttons: one with a red circle in the center, one with a square in the center, one with an arrow, and the last with a picture of a microphone. The red-circle button starts the recording; the square button stops it; the arrow button erases what was recorded; and the microphone button allows you to make sure the microphone is set up properly. You can get a microphone for the PC (or Mac)—they are inexpensive and are sold anywhere computer hardware is sold. Start by plugging in the microphone. If you then click on the microphone button, it will take you to the Sound Hardware Test Wizard. This will lead you through the process of making sure the microphone will work with the computer.

A Quiet Place to Record

The recording part can be a challenge, not because it's difficult but because unlike the other steps in this process, you can't have twenty students all recording their audio in the same room at the same time. You have to find a relatively quiet place— the microphones are pretty good at screening out noise—and record one student at a time. So, get some help if you can. Parents, aides, or students who are good with the technology can all help get the recording done. I've done recordings in guidance counselors' offices, teachers' lunchrooms, and a supply closet. The closet was right outside the auditorium where the chorus was rehearsing, so with some second graders' stories there's a little sound track that wasn't intended! But it didn't hurt the stories any.

The recording itself is easy. You click on the button with the red center to start recording; the button with the square on it to stop recording; the preview button to hear what you just recorded; and the arrow button if you want to erase what you recorded and do it over. Remember that students will record one piece of their story to go with each image, rather than recording the whole story in one big piece. This actually makes things easier because if a student makes a mistake or is unhappy with the quality of the recording, you can erase just one piece instead of having to do the whole thing over.

You'll see that on the film strip, when a student has recorded audio, a little balloon appears at the bottom of the picture the audio goes with to remind the student that he or she has recorded for that picture already.

You may want to talk with students about having expression and emphasis when reading and have them practice. I've had students practice out loud or read their script silently or both before they record. This is also a great way to see if the script works, if it really sounds the way a student wants it to. Often students hear a rough transition or word they don't like and change it before recording.

Third-grade teacher Debbie Finch does several different activities with her students to help them learn to read with expression. She models good reading; she has students read aloud and act out plays in class; she has students listen to one another read aloud and comment on their classmates' reading; and sometimes she facilitates a reader's theater where students take a story they've read and turn it into a play.

At the end of the digital storytelling process, she says, "the children read their story as they feel it should be read. They often feel a lot of ownership in this part [of the process]" (2009).

Narration, Music, and Revision

While students are recording the audio and creating the music, they will continue to proofread and revise, changing their text, correcting their captions, changing and resetting the music, and making sure the music is set to the right volume so the voice can be heard. I've actually seen students revising with glee and revising with great seriousness at these points in the process. As the whole comes together, as they can really see the pictures with the audio, they get a better sense of whether what they've written and what they've chosen for images go together well, whether they need to say more or less, and whether they need to show more or less with images. They may, at this stage, go back to collecting, adding to the text or looking for other images. Questions students can ask themselves to help with revision include these: Have I gotten my main message across clearly? Have I said what I wanted to stay? Will my audience understand everything in my story? Do the pictures and the text go together well? Is there anything I've left out? Is there anything I've included that doesn't need to be in the story? Is the story organized in a way that makes sense? Students might also share their stories at this point with their classmates to see whether they have any questions about them.

Adding Music

Not every teacher I worked with had students add music. It is something that will take more time. But it's also one more way students can think through their stories, so if you

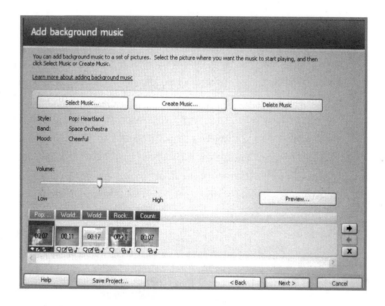

Figure 4.11 Add Background Music screen

Microsoft Digital Story 3 screen shots reprinted with permission from Microsoft Corporation.

can take the time, try it. Students can create their music before recording the audio. You'll find, though, that you'll probably have to go back and adjust the volume of the music so the voice-over can be heard.

As I mentioned in Chapter 2, students can download music from a CD or Web site to use with this program. If you have any musicians in your class, they might perform and be recorded for a story. Photo Story 3 also allows students to create music to go with their stories. They can create a different piece of music for each image, or one that runs through the whole story. They start by clicking on the Next button once recording is done.

When they've clicked from the Narrate Your Story and Customize Motion screen to the Add Background Music screen, they'll see a Select Music button and a Create Music button (see Figure 4.11). Select music is for music they've downloaded from a Web site or a CD.

To create original music for their stories, students click on the Create Music button; they'll get to another screen with options they can choose from (see Figure 4.12). They can choose a genre, such as pop; a style, such as pop R&B; instruments, under the Bands menu; and a certain mood, under the Moods menu. They can adjust the tempo so it's faster or slower and change the intensity of the music by choosing low, normal, or high. Increasing the intensity of the music makes it brighter and more complicated. Once they've created the music, they can play it, make changes, play it again, and so on. Then when they've got it where they want it, they can click OK and then try the Preview button so they can see how it goes with the images. If they want to make changes, they just choose Create Music again.

Suppose a student has three images and wants to have different music for each. When he or she creates the music for the first image, the program automatically runs the music across all three images. To create different music for the second image, the student should return to the Add Background Music screen, click on that image, click on Create Music, and go through the same process as before. To then add different music to the third image, he or she can click on that one and go through the process again.

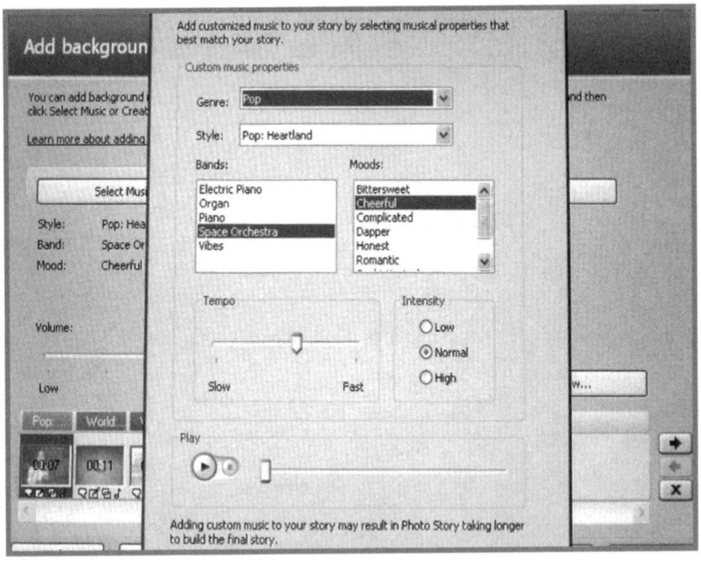

Here students should be thinking about the mood or tone of their stories, as well as what action is taking place. Will a fast tempo fit the story best, or a slow one? Classical music or carnival music? What will match up well with my words and pictures, rather than just being distracting?

Figure 4.12 Music options

Microsoft Digital Story 3 screen shots reprinted with permission from Microsoft Corporation.

As I mentioned, if students create their music before they do their recording, you're probably going to have to go back afterward and turn down the music volume, which you can do for each piece of music using the Add Background Music screen. Before they record their voices, the students don't know how loud or soft the music should be.

When they've got their stories just as they want them, it's time to finish the projects by turning them into Windows Media Video or *wmv* files.

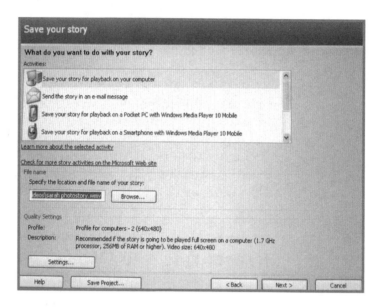

Figure 4.13 Save Your Story screen

Microsoft Digital Story 3 screen shots reprinted with permission from Microsoft Corporation.

Finishing the Digital Stories

Have students click the Next button to move from the Add Background Music screen to the Save Your Story screen (see Figure 4.13).

Here you'll usually want them to stay with the default option from the menu that says, "Save your story for playback on your computer," though there are other options they could use. The default will work if you're going to save the stories on the computer system and/or create CDs of the projects for the kids to take home. (You can also change the settings with the Settings button to get the best quality video picture possible, say, if you want to create a CD instead of a CD. Click on Help to get information on how to choose settings.) A student can use the Browse button to find the folder he or she wants to save the story in and name the story. Then the student can click on the Next button, and the computer will begin saving the story as a Windows Media file. It does not delete the original Photo Story 3 project file, so that will still exist.

Up until students save the projects as Windows Media files, they can view the stories only on a computer that has Photo Story 3 installed. After they save them as *wmv* files, they can watch them on any computer that has Version 7 or higher of the Windows Media Player.

If you want to create CDs or CDs for students, you'll need to see whether your computers have CD or CD burners and what software is installed. There are different programs out there; my computer, for instance, has the programs Windows CD Maker and Roxio Creator.

· · · · · · · · · · · · · · · · · · ·

Presenting the Work

After this, it's showtime. If you have a projector that hooks up to a computer, you can show the stories right off the computer, or burn a CD and play them off of that. You'll find students enjoy watching their own stories again and again, as well as those of others. Nobody should be forced to share his or her story, but I've never run into a student who didn't want it shown.

Digital stories can also be posted to a school's Web site. For one school I worked in, the principal televised students' digital stories on the local access channel. Other schools had fairs or viewings for parents.

However you do it, celebrate these stories with a showing. Let your young moviemakers enjoy their success.

Learning Through Digital Storytelling: Standards and Assessment

As they are searching the Internet for information [for digital stories], they can "bookmark" sites with good pictures to collect later. The goal I have for them . . . is to find a matching picture to support the text they have written. As they are sifting through for the best choices, they are doing a lot of evaluating and deeper thinking. They also experience how much junk is on the Internet and how to sort through and find what they need. Other skills they practice are classifying and organizing information, note taking, paraphrasing, proofreading, and editing.

—Joan Harris, fourth-grade teacher, Epping, New Hampshire

When third-grader Grace began her digital story about her dog Willow (see "Grace Willow" on CD), she chose to tell the story in Willow's voice, from Willow's point of view. She had to think about what in the world was most important to Willow and what details would set the dog apart from other dogs so the audience would stay interested. She also had to try to capture the way Willow would sound if she could talk. And Grace had to get the text to work with photographs and music in Photo Story 3. The result? A mischievous and enthusiastic dog telling us she's a black lab who wears "a vibrant blue collar," swims in rivers, and loves to eat. In the story Willow says, "Do you like dog treats? I do. They're the best . . . Sometimes I have to embark on a trip to the neighbor's cat food surplus because these people never give me enough food."

When fifth-grader Janki wrote her story about the Sahara Desert as a biome (see "Addax" on CD), she chose to tell about the addax, an antelope that is especially suited to living in the desert. She had to figure out what would be most important and most interesting to include in this short piece and what would give us a sense of what this biome is like. She also had to figure out how best to use her images and music. Her story? A minidocumentary about this creature of the desert, including intriguing information about how the endangered addax is one of the world's rarest mammals and numbers "close to just 250 in the wild." The story makes the audience want to know more about why this is so.

Standards

Grace and Janki practiced all sorts of skills while putting together their stories, skills that can fulfill language arts standards and technology standards. Given that teachers do not need one more thing to add to their list of what they must teach, it's important to realize that digital storytelling involves skills that some educational standards suggest students should master. It's not just an extra added on without connection to the curriculum.

Consider the language arts standards posted online by the National Council of Teachers of English and the International Reading Association (you can find the complete list of standards at www.ncte.org/standards). These standards include skills or tasks included in many state standards as well. The seven (out of twelve) NCTE/IRA standards that mesh with digital storytelling are as follows:

1.   *Students read a wide range of print and non-print texts to build an understanding of texts, of themselves, and of the cultures of the United States and the world; to acquire new information; to respond to the needs and demands of society and the workplace; and for personal fulfillment. Among these texts are fiction and nonfiction, classic and contemporary works.*

One nonprint text is the digital story. Before Grace and Janki wrote their stories, they watched digital stories by other students to get an idea of what was possible. Janki also used other print texts—Web sites—to gather information for her story.

4.   *Students adjust their use of spoken, written, and visual language (e.g., conventions, style, vocabulary) to communicate effectively with a variety of audiences and for different purposes.*

Viewers won't forget Willow once they meet her, because Grace grabs her audience's attention by including specific details that make Willow stand out, like the fact that this always-hungry dog likes apples. The photographs also pull you in and help tell the story; they include one of Willow with her head stuck deep inside a dog-biscuit box. Also, Grace uses certain language to get Willow's voice just right. Willow ends her story by saying, "I think I have a pretty sweet life. I have a big comfy bed. Do you think I have a pretty sweet life? I think that people should play with their dogs more."

Janki uses carefully chosen details to tell viewers what makes the addax special. Her narration works well with her pictures to tell the story of where and how the addax lives. At the end, Janki addresses her audience directly to leave them with one final thought connecting them to the story of the addax: "So if you go on a vacation to Africa, to the Sahara Desert, you may see an addax along your drive. And you may say, 'Hey, there's an addax.'"

6.   *Students apply knowledge of language structure, language conventions (e.g., spelling and punctuation), media techniques, figurative language, and genre to create, critique, and discuss print and non-print texts.*

Grace makes the text and the visuals work well together to build a portrait of her pet. She also makes good use of language when, on top of a picture of Willow eating, she adds text: "I LOVE FOOD." We definitely get the message! Janki's story also matches text to visual well, so that, for example, when she discusses how many young an addax produces, a picture of baby addaxes is displayed. Her language is clear and direct.

> 7. *Students conduct research on issues and interests by generating ideas and questions, and by posing problems. They gather, evaluate, and synthesize data from a variety of sources (e.g., print and non-print texts, artifacts, people) to communicate their discoveries in ways that suit their purpose and audience.*

Janki did Web research to gather the information and images for her story. She had to sort through the data she gathered to choose the most interesting or important information to include.

Grace evaluated the information she collected from observing Willow and figured out what to put in and what to leave out to best portray her dog in the story.

> 8. *Students use a variety of technological and information resources (e.g., libraries, databases, computer networks, video) to gather and synthesize information and to create and communicate knowledge.*

Janki used computers to gather information online but also to figure out how best to deliver that information. Grace used her photographs as a sort of outline for her story and had Willow chronicle all the things that make for "a pretty sweet life."

> 11. *Students participate as knowledgeable, reflective, creative, and critical members of a variety of literacy communities.*

Grace and Janki took part in such a community when they shared their stories, watched those of their classmates, and talked with them about what makes for a good digital story.

12. *Students use spoken, written, and visual language to accomplish their own purposes (e.g., for learning, enjoyment, persuasion, and the exchange of information).*

Clearly, that's just what Grace and Janki did.

Digital storytelling also meets technology standards. Some states now require students to compile digital portfolios; digital stories are perfect for the portfolios. States have set out other technology standards that call on students to demonstrate much the same skills as do the National Educational Technology Standards, or NETS, posted online (2007) by the International Society for Technology in Education (you can find the complete list of standards at www.iste.org/NETS).

Students creating digital stories often tackle much of what the NETS and other technology standards call for: creating something new with technology; using technology to think critically and solve problems; using technology to conduct research; understanding how the technology works; communicating with others using the technology; using the technology in an ethical manner.

Here are specific NETS that can relate to digital storytelling, depending on what kinds of writing and research students are doing:

Students:

1. *b. create original works as a means of personal or group expression.*

Grace and Janki have done so, using computers and Photo Story 3.

3. *a. plan strategies to guide inquiry.*
   b. locate, organize, analyze, evaluate, synthesize, and ethically use information from a variety of sources and media.

Both students went through a writing process to plan and draft their stories. Janki gathered information from several online resources and decided what was most significant and interesting.

4. *a. identify and define authentic problems and significant questions for investigation.*
b. plan and manage activities to develop a solution or complete a project.

Janki had to figure out what questions her digital story would answer. And, again, both students went through the writing process, planning and managing activities to complete their stories.

5. *a. advocate and practice safe, legal, and responsible use of information and technology.*

By discussing copyright issues and following fair-use guidelines, students are using the information they gather online legally and responsibly.

It's easy to demonstrate that students are doing much more than simply creating pretty slide shows when they're working on digital stories. They're practicing important skills and learning to think in meaningful ways about the process of writing and using technology to put the different elements of stories together.

● ● ● ● ● ● ● ● ● ● ●

Assessment

Assessing the writing for these projects is much like assessing any writing students do, but you may want to also consider the additional elements of digital stories such as voice-over, music, and images.

You can find many examples of rubrics for assessment online. Go to the Educational Uses of Digital Storytelling site (http://digitalstorytelling.coe.uh.edu) or the TechTeachers site (http://techteachers.com), and you'll find examples or links to examples. Do a search for "rubrics" and "digital storytelling" and you'll find more. Some were created with RubiStar (http://rubistar.4teachers.org), a Web site that offers free help for teachers creating rubrics.

Some rubrics concentrate on the seven elements that the Center for Digital Storytelling has said should be present in a digital story: a dramatic question, point of view, emotional content, economy, the gift of your voice, the power of the sound track, and pacing. These rubrics evaluate how well students employ each of the elements in their stories. You could certainly adapt such a rubric using the elements I describe in this book if you wished. You could also evaluate only the writing part of the project, which is what one teacher I met did. If you are going to create a rubric, you'll want to figure out exactly what you want the students to learn and demonstrate through these projects. Do you want them to learn how to use the seven elements? Are you having them conduct research and so need to assess that aspect of the project? What aspects of writing and storytelling have you discussed with students? What are you most interested in having students attempt when creating digital stories?

One third-grade teacher, Susan Carter, of Epping, New Hampshire, created the following rubric for her students:

4   *Mature: The writing is focused on a topic and supported with details and/or examples. The writing shows a clear beginning, middle, and end with ideas separated into paragraphs. Author's voice/personality contributes to the writing through effective word choice and varied sentence structure. Sentences are complete, and surface errors (spelling, grammar, punctuation) are minimal. Illustrations are well thought out, detailed, use color and enhance the story line.*

3   *Capable: The writing is focused on a topic and includes details. The writing shows a beginning, middle, and end; the writer may attempt to separate ideas into paragraphs. Author's voice/personality is evident through use of descriptive words and simple and compound sentences. Sentences are complete, and surface feature errors (spelling, grammar, punctuation) don't interfere with understanding. At least three out of the four items for illustrations are followed. (Illustrations are well thought out, detailed, use color and enhance the story line.)*

2   *Developing: Topic is presented but not developed; focus may wander. There is an attempt to organize ideas, but writing may lack connections. The writing may show limited vocabulary and/or simple*

sentence structure, but surface errors may make understanding difficult. At least two out of the four items for illustrations are followed. (Illustrations are well thought out, detailed, use color and enhance the story line.)

1   **Emerging:** Writing shows minimal focus on topic or is too limited in length. The writing shows little direction or organization. Vocabulary is limited and sentences are simple. Minimal control of surface features (spelling, grammar, punctuation) makes understanding difficult. At least one out of the four items for illustrations are followed. (Illustrations are |well thought out, detailed, use color and enhance the story line.)

This rubric clearly reflects the teacher's priorities in terms of writing and use of images. It seems like a framework her students would find easy to understand and use.

Another clear, specific rubric I found online was created with RubiStar by Kevin Hodgson, technology liaison for the Western Massachusetts Writing Project (http://www.umass.edu/wmwp/DigitalStorytelling/Rubric%20Assessment.htm). See Kevin's Digital Storytelling Rubric on the following page.

As you can see, in each category students can earn a certain number of points, which are then totaled for final scores.

You might also want to look on the Digitales site (http://www.digitales.us), where Bernajean Porter has created Digital Media Scoring Guides.

Rather than creating a rubric yourself, you might want to have your students come up with criteria for good digital stories through a group discussion, after they've watched some examples and talked about what they think works and what doesn't, what the stories' strengths and weaknesses are. These criteria could serve as a rubric.

Once the digital stories are done, it's helpful to give students a chance to reflect on the process as well as the product. Ask them what worked best for them, what they learned, what they struggled with, and what they'd do differently next time. This information will not only help you design their next digital storytelling project, but it will also show students how much they got out of creating their stories—how much they know after completing the stories that they didn't know before.

DIGITAL STORYTELLING RUBRIC

*Student Name:*_____

CATEGORY	20	15	10	5	Subtotal
Point of View— Purpose	Establishes a purpose early on and maintains a clear focus throughout.	Establishes a purpose early on and maintains focus for most of the presentation.	There are a few lapses in focus, but the purpose is fairly clear.	It is difficult to figure out the purpose of the presentation.	
Voice—Pacing	The pace (rhythm and voice punctuation) fits the story line and helps the audience really "get into" the story.	Occasionally speaks too fast or too slowly for the story line. The pacing (rhythm and voice punctuation) is relatively engaging for the audience.	Tries to use pacing (rhythm and voice punctuation), but it is often noticeable that the pacing does not fit the story line. Audience is not consistently engaged.	No attempt to match the pace of the storytelling to the story line or the audience.	
Images	Images create a distinct atmosphere or tone that matches different parts of the story. The images may communicate symbolism and/or metaphors.	Images create an atmosphere or tone that matches some parts of the story. The images may communicate symbolism and/or metaphors.	An attempt was made to use images to create an atmosphere/ tone but it needed more work. Image choice is logical.	Little or no attempt to use images to create an appropriate atmosphere/tone.	
Economy	The story is told with exactly the right amount of detail throughout. It does not seem too short nor does it seem too long.	The story composition is typically good, though it seems to drag somewhat or need slightly more detail in one or two sections.	The story seems to need more editing. It is noticeably too long or too short in more than one section.	The story needs extensive editing. It is too long or too short to be interesting.	
Grammar	Grammar and usage were correct (for the dialect chosen) and contributed to clarity, style, and character development.	Grammar and usage were typically correct (for the dialect chosen) and errors did not detract from the story.	Grammar and usage were typically correct but errors detracted from story.	Repeated errors in grammar and usage distracted greatly from the story.	

*Final Score:*_____

Afterword

It's time to give away the secret: teaching writing is fun.

—Don Murray, *A Writer Teaches Writing*

Everybody is a story.

—Rachel Naomi Remen, MD, *Kitchen Table Wisdom*

Have fun teaching digital storytelling. Writing sessions with students can be joyful and, during computer lab times, a little crazy—but good crazy, productive crazy. I've learned not just about the students' pets or pastimes but about how to listen to stories—quietly, waiting to be surprised.

I wish you the same marvelous experiences. The writing process model—and this book—isn't meant to be a rigid set of rules or steps teachers or writers have to follow. It offers guidelines, ways to talk and think about and practice writing. Feel free to adapt the process so it works for you and your students. Make it simpler or add more exercises to it. Let students bounce ideas off one another, help one another through the process. Enjoy their discoveries about what matters to them, what astonishes them, and what makes them wonder.

Last fall, while visiting one third-grade class, I talked with students as they were writing and sorting through photographs for their digital stories; I'd told them I was doing research for a book, and they were eager to help me out. Some were struggling with what they wanted to say in their stories, but they kept at the writing because they really wanted to tell and show these stories.

"What made you want to write about your sister's bunny?" I asked one young man. He said he thought it was cool that the bunny was friends with their cat. Another student told me she had decided to have her narrator be her dog to make the story more interesting; now she was trying to decide whether to record the narration in a gruff dog voice or her own. One student told me he'd included lots of questions in his story about a baseball game in which he was the pitcher—Would he throw a ball or a strike? Would he be the hero of the game?—so people would keep wondering what was going to happen next. Another explained that she was trying to describe her imaginary animal friend so others would understand what a funny character he was. Yet another was trying to figure out how best to explain all the things his older brother did to help him.

Every student I talked to was excited about these stories because they were going to be digital ones. No one asked me why I was writing a book about digital storytelling. They knew they were doing something book worthy.

I went back a couple of weeks later to help with the computer work. All of the students wanted me to come to their computers and see how their stories unfolded. When I left that day, the students were watching those stories, over and over again.

References and Resources

Finch, Debbie. 2009a. Personal communication. May 6.

———. 2009b. Personal communication. August 7.

Frazee, Marla. 2008. *A Couple of Boys Have the Best Week Ever.* Orlando, FL: Harcourt.

Gregg, Mary Jo. 2008. Class assignment. July.

Harris, Joan. 2009. Personal communication. June 9.

International Society for Technology in Education. 2007. *National Educational Technology Standards (NETS•S) and Performance Indicators for Students.* Eugene, OR: ISTE. Available online at http://www.iste.org/Content/NavigationMenu/ NETS/ForStudents/2007Standards/NETS_for_Students_2007_Standards.pdf.

Lambert, Joe. 2008. *Digital Storytelling: Capturing Lives, Creating Community.* 2nd ed. Berkeley, CA: Digital Diner.

Murray, Don. 1985. *A Writer Teaches Writing.* 2nd ed. Boston: Houghton Mifflin.

———. 1987. *Write to Learn.* 2nd ed. New York: Holt, Rinehart and Winston.

———. 2002. *Write to Learn.* 7th ed. Boston: Thomson Heinle.

———. 2005. *Write to Learn.* 8th ed. Boston: Thomson Wadsworth.

National Council of Teachers of English/International Reading Association. "Standards for the English Language Arts." NCTE. http://www.ncte.org/standards.

Ormiston, Meg, and Mark Standley. 2003. *Digital Storytelling with PowerPoint.* Eugene, OR: Visions—Technology Education.

Papazoglou, Ellie. 2009. Personal communication. March 9.

Project Tomorrow. 2005. *Our Voices, Our Future: Student and Teacher Views on Science, Technology and Education.* Irvine, CA: Project Tomorrow. Available online at http://www.tomorrow.org/speakup/pdfs/SpeakUpReport_05.pdf.

Remen, Rachel Naomi, M.D. 1996. *Kitchen Table Wisdom.* New York: Riverhead Books.

Rowling, J. K. 2000. Transcript of live interview. Scholastic.com. October 16. http://www2.scholastic.com/browse/article.jsp?id=10198.

Scieszka, Jon. 1989. *The True Story of the Three Little Pigs!* New York: Viking Penguin.

Sidman, Joyce. 2005. *Song of the Water Boatman and Other Pond Poems.* Boston: Houghton Mifflin.

Starr, Linda. 2004. "The Educator's Guide to Copyright and Fair Use." *Education World,* December 17. http://www.educationworld.com/a_curr/curr280.shtml.

Yolen, Jane. 1987. *Owl Moon.* New York: Philomel Books.

———. 2009. Interview by Claire E. White. *Writers Write: The Internet Writing Journal.* June 9. http://www.writerswrite.com/journal/jun02/yolen.htm.

Web Sites

Apple Learning Interchange—iLife in the Classroom
http://edcommunity.apple.com/ali/collection.php?collectionID=7

The Center for Digital Storytelling
http://www.storycenter.org

Classroom Clipart
http://classroomclipart.com

Classroom 2.0
http://www.classroom20.com

The Consortium of College and University Media Centers
http://www.ccumc.org

Digitales
http://www.digitales.us

Digital Storytelling in the Scott County Schools
http://www.dtc.scott.k12.ky.us/technology/digitalstorytelling/ds.html

Digital Storytelling Rubric by Kevin Hodgson
**http://www.umass.edu/wmwp/DigitalStorytelling/Rubric%20
Assessment.htm**

Discovery Education's Clip Art Gallery
http://school.discoveryeducation.com/clipart

EDTECH
http://www.h-net.org/~edweb

The Educational Uses of Digital Storytelling
http://digitalstorytelling.coe.uh.edu

Education World
"The Educator's Guide to Copyright and Fair Use"
http://www.educationworld.com/a_curr/curr280.shtml

FindSounds
http://www.findsounds.com

Freeplay Music
http://www.freeplaymusic.com

Integrating Digital Storytelling in Your Classroom
http://its.ksbe.edu/dst

Jordan School District Elementary Film Festival
http://t4.jordan.k12.ut.us/teacher_resources/film_festival.html

KitZu
http://www.kitzu.com

Microsoft
http://www.microsoft.com

The New York Public Library Digital Gallery
http://digitalgallery.nypl.org/nypldigital/index.cfm

Pics4Learning
http://pics4learning.com

RubiStar
http://rubistar.4teachers.org

Soundzabound
http://www.soundzabound.com

Tattle Tales
http://clow.ipsd.org/lmc_storytellers_Tattle_Tales_2005_2006.html

TechTeachers
http://techteachers.com

Index

Page numbers followed by an *f* indicate figures.